ELIMINATE STRESS FROM YOUR LIFE FOREVER

ELIMINATE STRESS FROM YOUR LIFE FOREVER

A Simple Program for Better Living

William Atkinson

American Management Association

New York • Atlanta • Brussels • Chicago • Mexico City • San Francisco
Shanghai • Tokyo • Toronto • Washington, D.C.

This publication is designed to provide accurate and authoritative
information in regard to the subject matter covered. It is sold with the
understanding that the publisher is not engaged in rendering legal,
accounting, or other professional service. If legal advice or other expert
assistance is required, the services of a competent professional person
should be sought.

Library of Congress Cataloging-in-Publication Data

Atkinson, William, 1951–
    Eliminate stress from your life forever : a simple program for better
living / William Atkinson.
        p.   cm.
    Includes index.
    ISBN 0-8144-7233-8
    1. Stress management.   2. Stress (Psychology)—Prevention.   3.
Relaxation.   I. Title.

RA785.A86   2004
155.9' 042—dc22   2003021523

Printing number

10   9   8   7   6   5   4   3   2   1

To my son, John,
who always helps me keep life in perspective

Contents

Foreword

Are you feeling stressed by your daily life and looking for ways to reduce or even eliminate stress altogether? The book you are holding right now is a great place to start. It will help you discover where your stress is coming from, motivate you to want to do something about it, and provide you with plenty of suggestions for how to deal with your stress in a healthier way.

As a registered dietitian in private practice, I meet stressed-out people every day. In fact, "emotional eating" is my specialty, and this is the phrase that often catches the attention of potential clients. We know we are stressed, but we are too overwhelmed to be able to do anything about it.

And that's where this book comes in! It will challenge you to examine your current sleep patterns, food choices, exercise habits, and relaxation techniques. It will help you sort out what areas of your life may be out of balance and causing your stress. And, it will motivate you to set a SMART (Small, Measurable, Attainable, Realistic, and Timely) goal each day for the next 100 days in those areas of your life where you are currently experiencing stress.

I know, I know, you don't have *time* to read a book about stress. My clients tell me this all day long. But what I really hear those clients saying is they don't *want* to take the time to take care of themselves. If you are ready to do something to reduce your current stress level and ultimately take better care of yourself, this book is a fantastic place to start!

Sharon Peterson, Ph.D., R.D., L.D.
Southern Illinois Nutrition Therapy

Preface

On September 21, 2000, the first day of autumn, I was playing Frisbee with my son on the road in front of our house. He made an errant throw, and the Frisbee began curving sharply and quickly toward our house, along the concrete driveway. Feeling particularly energetic that evening, I decided to give chase rather than allow it to fall harmlessly to the ground and have to retrieve it. I started running full speed toward it, moving closer and closer to the driveway. Unfortunately, I was wearing slip-on shoes, which should more rightfully have been called slip-off shoes since this was a much more common occurrence for them. As I raced across the lawn and neared the driveway, the left shoe slipped off. A thought passed through my mind: I ought to slow down and retrieve it. However, another thought passed through my mind at the same time: That would be difficult to do, because I'm moving way too fast.

For better or worse, my mind didn't have the opportunity to select either choice. At that moment, I passed the line between the lawn and the edge of the driveway. As I did so, my right shoe caught on the raised edge of the concrete and my body became airborne, rocketing upward at an angle through the air. However, gravity being what it is, that didn't last long, and my body descended just as quickly as it had ascended. I came crashing down on my right side—my hip first, knee second, shoulder third, and skull fourth. Then, everything went skidding across the concrete. I felt my skin rip in all four locations and knew I would be hurting when I arose.

A neighbor, walking his dog, looked at my plight with surprise and genuine concern, but I waved him off, yelling, "I'm OK!" Little did I know. I stood up quickly to brush myself off, but my body crumpled to the ground. "That's odd," I thought to myself. So I stood up again, and a third time. Each time, I crumpled to the ground, unable to put any weight on my right leg.

I admit: I am a slow learner. It took a while for the situation to sink in: I'd broken my hip. I crawled to the grass, which was softer albeit colder than the driveway, and lay there. By this time, my son had arrived, and I told him to go inside and have my wife call 911.

As I lay there waiting for the ambulance, I thought about the situation. I knew I was headed for surgery. I'd be spending three or four days in the hospital. I knew I'd be going through a lot of pain. I knew I'd have a lot of medical expenses, being self-employed with a "bread-and-butter" health insurance policy with a multi-thousand-dollar deductible. I knew I'd miss at least a couple of days of work, also a problem when you're self-employed and don't have anyone to pay your wages when you're not working. I also knew I'd have a very inconvenient and lengthy recovery period—more inconvenient for my family than for me in that it would require them to do quite a bit for me over the next few weeks or months.

At the same time, I was experiencing a feeling of total

calm—no stress of any kind. If this had happened a couple of years before, I know I would have been stressed—big time. Yet, a lot had changed in recent years.

Seven years earlier, I had begun a slow but definable spiritual journey that helped me begin to put life and all that related to it into perspective. On a more pragmatic level, I had been doing a lot of research in the area of stress management and interviewed a lot of experts in that field for articles I was writing for business magazines. As all of this was taking place, I was learning more about how to get rid of stress in my own life.

The topic became so interesting to me that as I was researching other topics for articles, I began to find some interesting, and heretofore undiscovered, links between them and stress. One related to the work of Martin Seligman on optimism and pessimism, and how the latter could lead to the concept of "learned helplessness." Another related to the work of a number of researchers on the concept of "risk taking"—why some people take risks that others would not, whether it be to snowboard off a mountain or drive recklessly while under the influence of illegal drugs. Still another area was the work of Al Siebert, a psychologist who had been studying "human resiliency." I was fortunate to be able to interview Al for a number of magazine articles on this topic.

What resulted was a completely new way of looking at the concept of stress and how to manage it. Although most writing on stress focuses on how to decompress from it after it's already taken hold of you, everything I was learning focused on how to prevent it from even occurring in the first place. I began synthesizing all of these concepts into my articles. At the same time, I began synthesizing the concepts into my own life. Without realizing it, the first time I really had the opportunity to put my newfound research and knowledge to the test was when I broke my hip. It obviously worked.

X-rays at the hospital did indeed confirm the fact that I had broken my hip. The orthopedic surgeon on call that evening came by my room to explain that he would be performing surgery in the morning, outfitting me with a contraption of steel plates, bolts, and screws that would set my broken bone and then remain in my body for the rest of my life.

I spent that evening and night lying in the hospital bed and again became aware of just how relaxed I was. I was experiencing total calm. I knew everything would be all right.

It's now over a year later and everything is, indeed, all right. The surgery was a success. My recovery, although long and painful, occurred without a hitch. I did miss a couple of days of work, but that was OK. The medical bills came in, but we had enough savings to cover them, and we have built that savings back up since then. Yes, there was a lot of physical pain over the ensuing days, weeks, and months, and there were a lot of inconveniences for my family members, who were very supportive. However, there was no emotional pain. There was no stress.

I usually keep my insights into life to myself, unless it seems clear that someone wants to hear them, which doesn't happen all that often, but that's OK. However, over the last several months, it has become abundantly clear to me that most people experience a lot of stress in their lives. I thought about offering some random tips to help them navigate these difficult experiences, but I realized that, given the complex causes of and solutions to stress, such casual comments would basically be worthless. I decided that it made a lot more sense to organize everything I had learned about stress into a book, and hope that the comprehensive information might offer some value to the reader.

ELIMINATE STRESS FROM YOUR LIFE FOREVER

Introduction

Another book on stress? What's the point? Indeed, there have been dozens of books written on coping with stress in recent years. Is there really a need for another one? There is if it's different, and this is different—very different—in a number of ways.

For better or worse, existing books on stress can be organized into three categories:

1. The majority of books focus on "decompressing" or "cleaning up" after the fact. That is, they provide information on how to get rid of stress after you've already been stressed: "Get a massage." "Take a walk." "Listen to music." That's like writing a book on cancer or heart disease and telling people how to live their lives as "cancer survivors" or "heart attack survivors" after they've already experienced the disease, rather than telling them what they can do to prevent the disease in the first place. Although books on "how to survive after the fact" are indeed important, books that show

1

you how to reduce your chances of ending up with the disease in the first place can be even more important. The book you are holding in your hands now works from the premise that stress is a brain-triggered illness, and it can be prevented!

2. A second category of books offers suggestions on how to manage and organize your life better in order to reduce stressful conditions. Although "life organization" is an important tool in overall stress management, it is only one of many tools. Improved life organization will help the average person eliminate maybe, at most, 10 to 20 percent of stress in his or her life.

3. The final category includes books that offer platitudes on how to pretend that stress doesn't even exist. Suggestions include ideas such as "Just think positive." That idea plus fifty cents will be enough to buy you a Hershey bar.

As someone who found himself easily stressed in various situations, but who spent years studying the habits of successful people who seemed consistently unfazed by stress, I am now living proof that stress can be eliminated. For example, despite the enormity of the tragedy, I experienced only mild discomfort after 9/11 and was back at work unruffled the very next day, although research conducted by a Dallas consulting firm showed that a majority of the nation's workforce was significantly stressed for two to three weeks following the attacks.[1]

More recently, a December 2001 Gallup Poll asked people how often they felt stressed on a daily basis. Results: Frequently (42 percent), Sometimes (38 percent), Rarely (18 percent), and Never (2 percent).[2]

How have I eliminated stress from my life? As a full-time business management writer for over twenty-seven years, I have had the opportunity to interview literally thousands of business and academic professionals. As part of many of these interviews, regardless of the article I was writing, I asked many of these people one final question: "How do you eliminate stress from your life?"

Over the years, I compiled the answers of hundreds of these people. I then spent several years studying the latest medical and psychological research on stress. The results led to some startling and, I believe, very original ideas about stress. These can be summarized into two general strategies that can help you prevent stress from taking over your life:

1. The type and amount of stress you experience is a direct result of your beliefs and attitudes. People who experience virtually no stress operate with different beliefs and attitudes than people who do experience stress. I have identified fourteen of these beliefs and attitudes, and every one of them can be changed.

2. The amount of stress you experience is also a direct result of your overall physical health. People who experience the least amount of stress are those who take great care to focus on four activities related to their health—sleep, nutrition, exercise, and relaxation.

Sleep. New research on sleep shows that the length and depth of sleep you get has a cyclical effect on stress. In sum, the more restful sleep you get, the less stressed you are. Subsequently, the less stressed you are, the easier it is to get more restful sleep. Conversely, people who are stressed tend to sleep poorly, and the lack of sleep reduces their abilities to cope with stress.

Nutrition. A tremendous amount of new medical research is showing that certain vitamins, minerals, and other supplements can chemically prevent the stress reaction from occurring in the body by reducing the creation of stress-producing hormones. Although some people have physiological systems that use vitamins, minerals, and other nutrients from food very efficiently (providing sufficient levels for stress prevention), most people have systems that use such nutrients less efficiently. As such, most people need additional amounts of certain vitamins, minerals, and other supplements to prevent physiological stress responses.

Exercise. The proper types of exercise can create physiological and chemical changes in the body that will help to reduce stress-producing hormones or prevent them from forming.

Relaxation. A tense body is stress's playground! When stress occurs, the body tends to tense up. Failure to reduce the tension encourages the stress response to continue. Thus, it is important to find ways to reduce physical tension in order to reduce stress. Two of the best ways to achieve this relaxation are meditation, which triggers physiological responses opposite those triggered by stress, and deep breathing, which slows down functions in the body that have been accelerated by stress.

Also new in this book is the idea that there are important links among:

- Stress and whether a person is an optimist or a pessimist
- Stress and a person's preferred level of risk taking
- Stress and how resilient a person tends to be

This book is divided into four parts. Part I focuses on the problems that stress can cause in your life (Chapter 1), how stress can be defined and categorized (Chapter 2), and the role of personality (attitudes and beliefs) in the creation of stress (Chapter 3).

Part II focuses on basic stress-prevention strategies, such as how diet, exercise, and sleep can build physiological and chemical barriers that will prevent, or at least reduce, your body's tendency to experience stress (Chapter 4); how to reformulate your attitudes and beliefs so as not to be affected by experiences that have traditionally stressed you (Chapter 5); and numerous other strategies to prevent or reduce stress in your life (Chapter 6).

Part III focuses on advanced stress-prevention strategies, such as building physical and mental energy via a Chinese exercise called chi kung (Chapter 7); how to understand and utilize the many benefits of meditation as both a stress-reduction and stress-prevention technique (Chapter 8); and the benefits of expanding your experience of life to include the spiritual realm, and why doing so may have the most profound impact on preventing stress in your life (Chapter 9).

Part IV provides details of a 100-day program you can follow that utilizes all of the recommendations offered in the book.

PART I

Stress: A Multidimensional Enemy

In Part I, we will look at what kinds of problems stress can cause in your life (Chapter 1). If you find yourself a victim of stress, it is important to realize that the mental frustration and pressure you experience are only the tip of the iceberg in terms of the problems that can occur as a result of the stress. Chronic stress can lead to a number of serious short-term and even long-term illnesses and diseases. This understanding alone should provide sufficient motivation to eliminate stress from your life.

We will also look at the categories and causes of stress to help you get a better understanding of where stress can originate in your life and how it occurs (Chapter 2).

Finally, we will look at the idea of "stress perception," related to stress personality, which suggests that the way you look at

what are considered the traditional causes of stress will determine, in large part, whether you actually experience the stress
response (Chapter 3). This chapter sets the stage for Part II,
which will look at a number of different ways to address stress in
your life.

CHAPTER ONE

When Your Body Wears Out, Where Are You Going to Live?

TIME magazine referred to stress as "America's #1 Health Problem."[1] Statistics bear out this claim:

- Northwestern National Life Insurance Company reported that 40 percent of workers say their jobs are "very stressful" or "extremely stressful."[2]

- The Princeton Survey Research Associates reported that 75 percent of employees believe workers today have more job-related stress than they did a generation ago.[3]

- The number of workers calling in sick due to stress tripled from 1996 to 2000.[4]

- According to the European Agency for Safety and Health at Work, more than half of the 550 million workdays lost each year are due to stress.[5]

- According to the American Institute of Stress, up to one million employee absences per day are stress related.[6]

▶ The American Institute of Stress reports that stress is a contributor to between 60 percent and 80 percent of all work-related injuries.[7]

▶ ManagedComp, a workers compensation insurer, reports that up to one-third of all workers compensation claims are attributable to job stress.[8]

▶ The American Institute of Stress reports that stress is a major factor in 40 percent of turnover.[9]

▶ The American Academy of Family Physicians estimated at one time that two-thirds of all family doctor visits are stress related.[10]

▶ By 1999, the American Institute of Stress reported that between 75 percent and 90 percent of primary-care physician visits had stress as a major contributing factor.[11]

▶ Research suggests that one of the keys to long life for centenarians (those living to 100 or older) is an ability to be minimally affected by stress. These are people who have an ability to handle new situations without undue tension.[12]

Effects of Temporary and Chronic Stress

Temporary (short-term) stress triggers the body to reach heightened awareness and preparation for action—commonly known as the "fight-or-flight" response. This response is biologically ingrained in us, as it was for our primitive ancestors, who needed it to respond to life-and-death situations.

Chronic (long-term) stress, however, causes the body to maintain this physiological reaction for long periods of time, which literally begins destroying the body. In his book *Ageless Body, Timeless Mind*, Deepak Chopra confirms that short-term stress leads to healthy arousal, while unrelenting stress leads to exhaustion, the results of which closely mimic those of the aging process, such as hypertension, ulcers, impotence, wasted muscles, diabetes, reduced disease resistance, and senility.[13]

Consider the following example: You're driving along a highway and ready to pass a vehicle in front of you. Just as you move into the oncoming lane, you see a car from the opposite direction coming over the hill toward you. You punch the accelerator, which guns the engine, sending you racing forward at a high speed. This extra power allows you to pull back into your lane in time. Your engine settles back to its normal speed. This is temporary stress.

Now consider this scenario: You punch the accelerator the moment you get on the highway and "put the pedal to the metal" for the whole trip. Don't expect to make it to your destination. If you don't crash first, your engine will explode from the unrelenting pressure. This is chronic stress.

How does chronic stress negatively affect your health? It can do so in four ways:

1. It can impose long-term wear and tear on your body, reducing its resistance to disease, including cancer.
2. It can directly precipitate illness, from headaches to heart attacks.
3. It can aggravate existing illnesses, such as arthritis.
4. It can precipitate unhealthy (illness-generating) habits, such as smoking, drinking, overeating, and not getting enough sleep.

Stress Hormones

The body's endocrine system consists of a number of glands, which secrete hormones. The most important glands in terms of stress are the adrenals: the adrenal medulla and the adrenal cortex. They release hormones that help prepare the body for a short-term heightened state of arousal (fight or flight).

The adrenal medulla releases epinephrine (adrenaline), norepinephrine (noradrenaline), and dopamine, all of which are necessary to achieve a heightened state of readiness. Prolonged secretion of these hormones, however, eventually depletes and wears out the adrenal medulla. The adrenal medulla can be depleted, and the end result is death.

The adrenal cortex, located near the liver, releases glucocorticoids and mineralocorticoids. The primary glucocorticoid is cortisol, which increases the body's energy by utilizing existing glucose (from the liver), fatty acids (from adipose tissue), and amino acids (from muscle). Prolonged stress, however, leads to nonstop secretion of cortisol, which causes fatigue, reduces antibodies (thus lowering the immune system's ability to resist disease), and increases the fatty acids circulating in the bloodstream (thus promoting atherosclerosis, which is fatty plaque buildup in the arteries).

The primary mineralocorticoid is aldosterone, which prepares the muscles for activity by retaining extra sodium, which leads to water retention. Prolonged stress, however, eventually leads to high blood pressure from the excess sodium and water retention, placing the cardiovascular system in danger.

Physiological Effects of Chronic Stress

If you suffer from chronic stress, you leave yourself open to a vast number of significant conditions, illnesses, and diseases, including cardiovascular disease, brain atrophy, reduced disease immunity, cancer, diabetes, excess body fat, muscle pain, bone loss, nutrient depletion, anxiety and depression, accelerated aging, other afflictions, and even sudden death!

Cardiovascular Disease

A recent study at Ohio State University found an increased risk of cardiovascular disease among people experiencing even mild chronic stress. The primary reason is explained in the previous section on adrenal functions. Stress can also lead to increased levels of:

▶ *Cholesterol.* One study showed a 20 percent increase in cholesterol levels of people during stressful work times.[14]

▶ *Triglycerides.* One study found that stress caused triglycerides to stay in the bloodstream longer.[15]

▶ *Homocysteine.* This is an amino acid that is strongly associated with cardiovascular diseases because it damages arterial walls.

Stress can also lead to cold hands and feet due to restricted circulation, and it can cause shortness of breath, placing additional strain on the cardiopulmonary (heart-lung) system.

Brain Atrophy

In her book *Your Miracle Brain*, Jean Carper reported on studies indicating that chronic stress can alter the structure and functioning of brain cells, leading to gradual brain damage and atrophy via the creation of free radicals. She reported on another study implicating stress in the death of the nerve cells that are responsible for memory. The loss, the study suggested, looked like the "death of neurons after a stroke or seizures."[16]

In fact, stress actually reduces the size of the hippocampus portion of the brain, which is responsible for memory. This is the result of the shrivelling of dendrites, which are the brain's communication pathways.

Reduced Disease Immunity

Again, the mechanisms for this are discussed earlier in the stress hormones section. One point of elaboration: The adrenal cortex releases significantly fewer T lymphocytes (antibodies) when the body is experiencing stress. These antibodies are instrumental in searching out foreign antigens that can cause infection.

Cancer

One cause of cancer is related to a suppressed immune system (discussed immediately above). That is, stress contributes to cancer by weakening the immune system, which is instrumental in defending the body against malignant cells. The body's natural killer (NK) cells, which are designed to destroy cancer cells, are weakened and suppressed during stress.

Diabetes

As noted in the section on the adrenal glands, stress leads to increased levels of cortisol in the body. Cortisol leads to an elevation in blood glucose. In response, the body's beta cells produce insulin. During periods of chronic stress, the beta cells eventually burn out and cannot be replaced. As a result, the body's ability to produce insulin is compromised, potentially leading to diabetes.

Excess Body Fat

Stress can cause general weight gain. This can occur in two ways. First, increased levels of cortisol and insulin send a signal to fat cells to retain their stores of fat. Second, increased cortisol levels increase food cravings, especially for carbohydrates. The reason is that stress reduces levels of serotonin (a "feel-good" neurotransmitter) in the body. Low levels of serotonin can lead to depression, which encourages the body to crave more carbohydrates to replace the serotonin (since carbohydrates are a major source of serotonin).

Although many people store fat in the buttocks, others store it in their abdomens. In fact, if you watch your calories and exercise regularly but still suffer from excess body fat in your stomach area, chances are this is "stress fat." Again, the culprit is excess levels of cortisol. In one study, subjects who ate sensibly and exercised but had previously been unable to get rid of the "belly bulge" were able to do so when they found ways to reduce stress in their lives.[17] (For more information on stress fat, get a copy of *Fight Fat After Forty.*)

Muscle Pain

Chronic stress can lead to muscle tightness, pain, and spasms. It can also lead to increased risk of developing back and upper-extremity musculoskeletal disorders as well as chronic lower back pain. Along the same lines, stress can trigger migraine headaches and tension headaches.

For example, I find it interesting to note that although the majority of drivers in the region where I live tend to be very polite and relaxed, those leaving the parking lot of a local chiropractor's office seem to be very tense and frustrated. They frequently impulsively shoot out into traffic on the main street at high rates of speed, often forcing other drivers to jam on their brakes to avoid collisions. I suspect the main reason these people are visiting a chiropractor is muscle pain, and the primary cause of the muscle pain may be stress, as evidenced by their driving behaviors.

Bone Loss

Bones are the repository for the body's calcium supply. Gluco-corticoids disrupt the natural flow of calcium to and from the bones. If the bones release too much calcium, they become fragile and prone to fracture. In addition, excess circulating calcium can start forming kidney stones.

Nutrient Depletion

Chronic stress can lead to depletion of vital nutrients in the body, particularly DHEA, vitamin C, and many of the B-complex vitamins. It should come as no surprise that cortisol, again, is implicated.

DHEA, a hormone that is particularly important for health and longevity, is a precursor to adrenaline and cortisol, which are released during stress. That is, each time the body is subjected to stress, it uses up its DHEA supply to create the adrenaline and cortisol. New research is showing that as people age, DHEA levels decrease, and this depletion is one reason for the aging process. In sum, the more you experience stress, the more quickly you age! One interesting study showed that men who meditate on a regular basis (a proven strategy for reducing stress) have 23 percent more DHEA than men who don't meditate, and women who meditate have 47 percent more DHEA than women who don't.[18]

Cortisol also depletes the body's reserves of vitamin C and the B-complex vitamins, which are necessary to maintain proper functioning of the nervous system and the endocrine system.

Anxiety and Depression

More and more research is showing that the shortage of certain vital nutrients (vitamins, minerals, etc.) can be a significant cause of anxiety and depression. Since stress depletes these supplies, those experiencing stress become more prone to subsequent anxiety and depression.

Accelerated Aging

In his book *Why Zebras Don't Get Ulcers*, author Robert Sapolsky notes that stress can become a vicious cycle in that:

▶ People lose the ability to cope with stress as they age. In fact, aging can be defined as the progressive loss of ability to deal with stress, physically and mentally. For example, when stressed, young people and older people will both exhibit signs of stress, but stress will generally be more pronounced in the older people, and the effects will remain longer. That is, secretions of epinephrine, norepinephrine, and glucocorticoid continue longer in the bodies of older people than they do in younger people. In fact, in some older people, secretions of these substances continue unabated (albeit at lower levels) even when the individuals are not even experiencing stress. These elevated levels may have a lot to do with elevated blood pressure levels seen in older people.

▶ Stress can accelerate the aging process.[19] According to Sapolsky, elevated glucocorticoid levels are the major cause of death in certain species of animals. When the adrenal glands are removed in these older animals (preventing additional secretions of glucocorticoid), the aging process slows and the animals don't die as quickly.

The locus of control for glucocorticoid secretions is the hippocampus portion of the brain. As people age, the hippocampus loses large numbers of neurons. As such, it loses some of its ability to regulate glucocorticoid secretion levels, allowing them to continue unabated. This leads to a vicious cycle, because glucocorticoid secretions are actually part of the cause of hippocampal damage. In other words, as the hippocampus sustains damage, more glucocorticoids are released, leading to more damage, and so on. In sum, the more stress you allow into your life, the more you open yourself to suffering from stress-related illnesses as you age.

Other Afflictions

Stress is implicated in gastrointestinal disorders (including indigestion, diarrhea, and constipation), occasional and chronic insomnia, and rheumatoid arthritis. It can even increase the likelihood of fatal asthma attacks in people who have asthma.

Stress can also lead to sexual dysfunction in men since increased levels of adrenaline and cortisol lead to decreased levels of testosterone. In one study, men who experienced the least arousal while viewing erotic movies were also those with the highest levels of cortisol.[20]

In women, stress can suppress ovulation. In one study, infertile women who had tried every high-tech fertility procedure possible participated in a stress-management group therapy session and learned additional relaxation response techniques. Within six months, half of them were pregnant.[21]

Last but not least, stress can increase cases of adult acne and also promote cavities by producing saliva containing proteins that encourage plaque formation, a bacterial coating that can lead to cavities.

Death by Stress

In the book *Is It Worth Dying For?* the authors report on life (and death) among employees at Florida's Cape Canaveral.[22] Due to stress associated with job uncertainties and the possibility of unemployment, compounded by chronic stress on the job, workers there at the time led the nation in drinking, drug use, divorce, and sudden heart attacks. Autopsies of workers who dropped dead without warning revealed that levels of adrenaline, cortisol, and other hormones were released into their bodies with such force that the hormones actually ruptured the muscle fibers of the heart.

One study discussed over 250 cases of people who died suddenly within minutes or hours of major events, with most of the people being in good or at least fair health prior to the events.[23] The authors identified four causes. One was traumatic disruption of close human relationships, such as the death of a loved one (135 deaths). The second was danger, struggle, or attack (103 deaths). Third was loss of status, self-esteem, or valued possessions; or disappointment, failure, defeat, or humiliation (21 deaths). Fourth was triumph, public recognition, reunion, or happy ending (16 deaths).

The fourth area is particularly interesting, emphasizing that even excessive positive stress can be a killer. For example, within hours of a fifty-five-year-old man's reunion with his eighty-eight-year-old father following a twenty-year separation, both men collapsed and died.

Summary

In this chapter, you learned that although your body ratchets up your system to cope with temporary stress, it experiences fatigue when faced with chronic stress. That is, if your life is racked with chronic stress, then stress is more than just a mental nuisance. It has serious implications that can lead to illness and disease—both in the short term and the long term. These can include cardiovascular disease, brain atrophy, reduced disease immunity, cancer, diabetes, excess body fat, muscle pain, bone loss, nutrient depletion, anxiety and depression, accelerated aging, other afflictions, and even sudden death.

CHAPTER TWO

Slicing and Dicing Stress— Categories, Causes, and Perceptions

To better grasp the concept of stress, it is important to understand the various categories, causes, and perceptions of stress.

Categories of Stress

Stress can be categorized in at least three different ways.

Type (Positive and Negative)

Positive Stress. Sometimes called "eustress," positive stress is helpful arousal that promotes health, energy, and peak performance. An example is stress associated with athletic training.

Negative Stress. Sometimes called "distress," negative stress is associated with too much or too little arousal resulting in harm to the mind and/or body.

Duration (Temporary and Chronic)

Temporary Stress. This is stress that does not last very long. Examples include stress as a result of a gunshot that goes off when you are in a large crowd or the "big boss" visiting you from out of town for the day.

Chronic Stress. This is stress that remains with you, such as experiencing continued stress days or weeks after the gunshot went off in the large crowd, or having to deal with a boss every day who makes your life miserable.

In most cases:

▶ Temporary positive stress is good, in that it encourages you to reach a state of valuable readiness that will help you in life.

▶ Chronic positive stress is extremely rare. It may manifest itself, for example, in people with extreme religious fervor.

▶ Temporary negative stress is useful in that it encourages you to reach a state of valuable readiness that can protect you from danger.

▶ Chronic negative stress has no value at all. This is the type of stress that is killing people today.

Time (Past, Current, and Future)

Past Stress. Sometimes called "residual stress," this is stress from the past, such as post-traumatic stress disorder. This is stress you cannot seem to let go of, even though the event that triggered it has long passed.

Current Stress. This is a state of arousal during an existing situation. Examples can include situational stress (something that requires your attention immediately, but that you do not enjoy having to address), encounter stress (having to deal with someone you'd rather not have to deal with), and time stress (having too little time to complete tasks or other responsibilities). Although much of what is classified as current stress is also temporary stress, it can also be chronic stress, such as stress experienced from the recent loss of a loved one, a recent accident or illness, or the loss of a job.

Future Stress. Sometimes called "anticipatory stress" or "worry," future stress is arousal over the future or worry about what might happen. Residual stress can also lead to future stress, such as when people who experienced a trauma in the past worry about whether it might occur again.

Causes of Stress

There are numerous ways to identify and categorize the causes of stress. Probably the simplest and easiest way to comprehend stress is to categorize the causes into five groupings: adaptation stress, overload stress, underload stress, frustration stress, and noise stress.

Adaptation Stress

This is by far the most pervasive cause of stress. The body and mind tend to prefer a state called "homeostasis"—the state in which the body exists in stable equilibrium. Excessive change in a person's life destroys homeostasis, forcing the body to use "adaptation"—the tendency to try to restore homeostasis when it is upset.

Probably the most well-known measure of adaptation stress is the Social Readjustment Rating Scale (SRRS), first published in 1967 by Holmes and Rahe.[1] The scale had 43 items (later revised to 63), with each item being given a weight based on its perceived severity and duration (which were tested on a sample population).

The scale addressed both positive and negative events, claiming that any significant change, whether positive or negative, would upset the body's homeostasis. Each weighting unit was called a Life Change Unit (LCU).

The most heavily weighted was the death of a spouse (100 LCUs). The lowest was a minor violation of the law, such as a traffic ticket (11 LCUs). The authors suggested that anyone with a score of 150 to 300 over a six-month period stood a 50 percent chance of falling seriously ill within that time frame. Anyone who scored above 300 stood an 80 percent chance of falling seriously ill.

The SRRS has been tested over the last several decades and seems to continue to be a valid predictor of how emotions related to LCUs will affect a person's health.

The SRRS's top ten are:

1 —	Death of Spouse	100
2 —	Divorce	73
3 —	Marital Separation	65
4 —	Jail Term	63
5 —	Death of Close Family Member	63
6 —	Personal Injury or Illness	53
7 —	Marriage	50
8 —	Fired at Work	47
9 —	Marital Reconciliation	45
10 —	Change in Health of Family Member	44

Despite the purported accuracy of the SRRS, other research-ers in recent years have suggested that it is life's daily hassles, even minor ones, that play a more significant role in determining stress-related ill health. That is, other research suggests that the most serious stress problems are those resulting from chronic stress (those that occur frequently or have a long duration), rather than those resulting from onetime events (those based on the severity of the stressor).

A number of lists of chronic stressors have been published over the years, and most of them end up finding these six to be the most common, in order of magnitude:

1 — Money
2 — Career or Job
3 — Health
4 — Sex and/or Conflicts in Marriage
5 — Conflicts and/or Problems with Children
6 — Time and/or Excess Responsibilities

Overload Stress

The second most common cause of stress is that related to over-load or overstimulation. These are situations where the demands placed on you (or demands that you place on yourself) exceed your capacity to meet those demands. The excess stimulation and expectations can lead to tension, anxiety, and confusion. The overload can occur at home, at work, at school, or a combination of these, and possibly even other places.

Underload Stress

Often called "deprivational stress," this is much less common and usually less serious than overload stress. In a technical sense, underload stress involves actual sensory deprivation (reduction in sight, touch, sound, smell, or taste).

On a more realistic level, it refers to people who are lonely and/or bored with life—people who have insufficient stimulation in life to find it interesting and exciting. Examples can include people who live alone and have no friends or people who work assembly line or other repetitive jobs.

One of the most interesting studies on deprivational stress took place at McGill University (Montreal) in 1954.[2] Volunteers received twenty dollars a day (a decent sum back then) to lie in a bed with their basic needs being met. However, the beds were in individual cubicles, and the volunteers' arms and hands were padded. In addition, they were required to wear goggles through which they could not see. Outside noise was masked by a speaker system. In sum, the volunteers were deprived of virtually all of their senses.

Most slept for the first few hours and enjoyed the relaxation. Soon, though, most began to experience boredom, restlessness, and anxiety. Some tried to stimulate themselves by singing, whistling, and talking to themselves, but nothing seemed to work. Eventually, those who remained began to suffer from unsettling, and even terrifying, experiences and hallucinations. Most of the volunteers quit after twenty-four hours, and no one lasted beyond seventy-two hours. (For more details on the implications of this fascinating study, see Chapter 8.)

Frustration Stress

This is stress associated with having natural or desirable behaviors or goals thwarted or inhibited.

Examples of personal frustration stress are being stuck in traffic, being stuck in a long line, and being unable to get through to someone on the phone because of a busy signal.

Examples of social frustration stress can include overcrowded living or working conditions, discrimination, and bureaucracy.

Noise Stress

Noise can produce stress in three ways:

1. It can overstimulate the sympathetic nervous system.
2. It can be annoying and subjectively displeasing.
3. It can disrupt attention to activities in which the person is engaged.

Perceptions of Stress

Up to this point, most of the information we have covered related to categories and causes of stress has been common knowledge. Here's where it starts to get interesting.

One of the most surprising realizations for people when it comes to learning about stress is that *there are no such things as stressors*. Stress is a perception—an attitude—a personal reaction to certain events. In sum, the same experience that stresses one person might positively invigorate someone else, and an event that paralyzes one individual might inspire another.

Take the example of skydiving: Although some people would probably suffer heart attacks if forced to skydive, others voluntarily do so for fun.

Although this is a little-known fact about stress, the idea that stress depends on perception is not new. Some philosophers figured it out centuries ago:

> ▶ "People are disturbed not by events, but by their view of those events." (Epictetus)

- "There is nothing either good or bad, but thinking makes it so." (Shakespeare)

- "The mind is its own place, and in itself can make a Heaven of Hell, a Hell of Heaven." (John Milton)

To elaborate: there are no stressors. It's just stuff happening. The distress that a person may feel is not a result of what actually and objectively exists. It is a result of how the person perceives what is happening. Stressors are not "out there" like invisible piranha ready to bite us at a moment's notice. Rather, stress is a reaction to a situation, and everyone reacts differently.[3] Let's look at the five causes of stress discussed earlier and see how they are not, in reality, stressors.

Adaptation

Looking at Holmes and Rahe's SRRS, one might argue that the death of a spouse (number one on the SRRS) could be a stressor for one person and a relief for another. If a young spouse dies suddenly and violently in an accident, one might expect the other spouse to experience significant stress. However, if a spouse has been afflicted with Alzheimer's for a decade and been unable to communicate with the other spouse for several years, and if the other spouse has been forced to readjust his or her life to take care of the daily needs of the afflicted spouse, then that spouse's death, although it may be stressful to a degree, might be more of a relief.

Take another example—fired at work (number eight on the SRRS): A person who fully planned to spend his whole life with a company; just took out a large mortgage on a house; has no savings; and has a wife, three children, and twins on the way would be extremely stressed if he were terminated. However, a young upstart who started working for a company out of college, who has no family and no debt, who quickly realized he couldn't stand his job because he's in the wrong line of work, and who couldn't wait for the opportunity to follow his dream of self-employment might actually be relieved, even elated, about being terminated.

Overload

As is the case with adaptation stress, overload stress is a perception:

Example: Take a room half filled with older employees who are ready to retire and half filled with young employees just out of college. Then, announce that you're going to introduce a new computer system on Monday morning, complete with the latest "bells and whistles." What will happen? Likely, the older employees, who took years to become comfortable with the existing system, will groan and immediately feel stress. "Why can't you just wait until we retire?" they will exclaim. The younger employees, on the other hand, who grew up with computers, will likely jump for joy, excited about the possibilities the new system will offer.

Now take another example, using the same people: Let's say that a major crisis hits the office one day. What will happen? Likely, the young employees, who have never experienced such a situation, will immediately experience stress. The seasoned veterans, on the other hand, will probably take control, address the situation, and calmly explain, "We've dealt with this before." They will gain feelings of pride and self-esteem at their ability to show the youngsters how things are done and mutter under their breaths to each other, "Computer wimps!"

Underload

Underload or deprivational stress suggests that people get stressed with too little stimulation. Maybe. Maybe not. Place your average Wall Street or Madison Avenue senior executive in a small town for two months with no computer, no cell phone, and no other communication technology and he might commit suicide. Yet, consider the fact that millions of people live in small towns and would have it no other way. In fact, some even live in cabins hidden from view on dirt roads. To these people, Wall Street and Madison Avenue would be the place to commit suicide.

Frustration

Stress researchers have suggested that problems such as overcrowding and discrimination are examples of frustration stress.

Yet what is overcrowding? Some people living in the Yukon wilderness would consider a small town overcrowded. People in the small town would consider New York overcrowded. Some people prefer to hike in the woods to unwind. Others prefer to go to crowded bars or dance clubs with loud music to unwind.

Discrimination? In and of itself, it is not a stressor. I recall traveling throughout the Deep South in the 1960s with friends from college. At the time, I had shoulder-length hair and a beard. This was before interstate highways and before every well-known country-western singer had long hair and a beard. This was the time when the only place southerners had seen hippies was on TV.

We stopped at roadside diners in small towns to eat, and I would never be served. I'd sit at a table with my friends, all of whom had short hair and were clean shaven, and a sullen waitress would take their orders, but not mine. My friends always ordered extra for me. Was I stressed by the discrimination or by the looks of hatred in the eyes of the other patrons? Not at all. I found the situation immensely amusing. What I enjoyed most was leaving a huge tip on the table (such as five dollars, when fifty cents was common at the time), then getting up after eating, passing the waitress wearing a big smile on my face, and saying, "Thank you!" What I wanted to do was force her and the others in the diner to rethink their attitudes—to try to get past their ignorance, which was no fault of their own. In sum, what I experienced was the opposite of stress.

Noise

Again, reaction to noise is attitudinal. Although some people would love nothing more than to spend an evening in the front row of an ear-shattering punk rock concert, others would probably experience heart failure.

Another example: I can't work without music. When my office is silent, I become totally distracted and tense. Once music is playing, I can once again settle in and concentrate on what I am doing. However, I've talked with other writers who can only work in total silence.

Summary

In this chapter, you learned that there are numerous categories of stress, which can be organized by type (positive, negative), duration (temporary, chronic), and time (past, current, future).

There are also a number of causes of stress including adaptation stress, overload stress, underload stress, frustration stress, and noise stress. Finally, there are a number of perceptions of stress, which allow you to look at all of the causes of stress in a new way.

CHAPTER THREE

The Stress Personality

As noted in the last chapter, stress is a perception rather than a universal reality. Whether you are stressed by a certain situation depends on how you view that situation. And how you view the situation will be determined largely by fourteen factors, which fall into two broad categories. These categories are what will determine your attitude toward, and perception of, a specific event or situation:

1. Your assessment of the situation (seven factors)
2. Your assessment of yourself (seven factors)

Assessment of the Situation

There are seven factors related to your assessment of a situation that will determine whether you experience stress, and, if you do, how much stress you will experience.

Knowledge

To put it bluntly, "Ignorance is bliss." If you are in the midst of a dangerous situation, but have no idea that it is dangerous, you will not experience any stress unless and until someone tells you that you are in danger.

When I was a child growing up in the Canadian Rocky Mountains in the early 1950s, my parents would often take me on wilderness hikes in the mountains. Once, we were surrounded by a half dozen bighorn sheep, which lived wild in the area. My parents were enthralled by the experience and took a number of photos, which I still have to this day. It was only later, when relating the experience to some friends, that they found out just how lucky we were. The bighorns were not only wild, but they were dangerous. It was not uncommon for them, when approached by humans, to attack. Upon learning this alarming information, my parents experienced stress.

In the 1960s, as a teenager living in a suburb north of Chicago, I frequently took the subway downtown. From there, I would walk four or five miles through what were, unbeknownst to me at the time, some of the worst and most dangerous areas of Chicago. These sections were north, west, and south of the Loop area. My reasons? I just loved to explore. I would always find unique shops, restaurants, and other places of interest. One particularly dangerous route led to Old Town, the "hippie hangout" in the 1960s. I specifically recall one chilly Saturday afternoon being caught in a downpour of rain on a side street a mile or two southwest of Old Town. It was an incredibly run-down neighborhood. As I walked along the sidewalks, I saw dozens of people staring at me out of their windows, wondering what that "crazy white kid" was doing in their neighborhood in the rain. The area was so isolated that I suspect some of the young children had never seen a white person before, other than on TV. I had dozens of these adventures from age fourteen through eighteen and never experienced any problems of any kind. It was only years later that I began to reflect on the potential danger in which I had continually been placing myself. At the time, though, not being aware of this, I experienced no stress of any kind. All I ever experienced was excitement and curiosity.

Responsibility

The level of stress you experience from a situation will also be based partially on how much responsibility you had for either creating the situation or currently have for addressing it, or, more specifically, how much responsibility you believe you have.

Example: A salesperson loses his largest account because the customer did not receive an important document in the mail and a follow-up informational phone call in time for an important project. Who gets stressed? The salesperson probably experiences the most stress, since his job is on the line. His boss, the sales manager, probably experiences some stress, too. The sales office's secretary? Probably not much stress at all—unless this was the person who was supposed to mail the document and make the phone call for the salesperson, but forgot to do so!

Conscientiousness

The more conscientious you tend to be, the more likely it is that you will experience stress when faced with a lengthy, complex, and/or new set of responsibilities.

For example, if you need to make twenty phone calls in the next two hours and get information from as many of the people you call as possible, you will likely experience a significant amount of stress if you are a conscientious person. The reason is that you will expect yourself to reach all of these people, and you will become upset if you are unable to do so. Someone who is much less conscientious may take the attitude of, "Well, I'll call them all. If I get through to them, fine. If not, it's not my fault. My boss should have given me more advance notice."

Caring and Value

The less value a situation has to you, the less you probably care about it. The less you care about, the less you will probably be stressed by it.

Example: You're in an automobile accident. You get stressed. Your neighbor is in an automobile accident. You may get stressed, but certainly not as much. Someone in another city whom you don't even know is involved in an automobile accident. You will probably not be the least bit stressed.

Enjoyment

How much you enjoy a particular situation or event will also determine how much you get stressed by it, or whether you get stressed at all. This is particularly true of jobs.

Example: If you love people and are a receptionist in the lobby of an electric utility office, you may love your job.

But let's say that the utility company wants to make some changes. It wants you to become a member of a line crew that climbs hundred-foot-high transmission towers and repairs multi-thousand-volt electric lines. Stress? You bet! Yet, there are workers who absolutely love this type of work. In fact, they go to school specifically to learn how to become part of a utility line crew. So what would happen if you forced one of them off the towers and into the office lobby to answer phone calls and greet customers? He or she would likely experience major stress.

Another example: A study of corporate purchasing managers conducted by a consulting firm found that approximately one-third of the managers were unhappy in their jobs and wanted to leave.[1] The primary reason they wanted to leave was job stress. They identified the two most prevalent stressors as "constant problems" and "constant change." Another third of the managers were comfortable in their jobs. The remaining third loved their jobs. The two things they loved most about their jobs? You guessed it: the constant challenges and the opportunity for change.

Control

Control refers to the freedom to make choices related to an event or situation. More specifically: How much freedom do you have to prevent, lessen, change, or terminate the severity of a negative event or situation? It is important not to confuse freedom with ability. Control relates to the *freedom* or *opportunity* to do something. Ability refers to your *competence* to do something. This is discussed later.

An example of how control affects stress levels: A study during World War II found that soldiers who had the opportunity to return enemy fire suffered fewer mental disorders than those who did not have the opportunity to return the fire, and who were instead forced simply to take shelter and hope they would not be harmed.[2]

As with responsibility, a critical issue with control is not only how much control you have, but how much control you believe you have. This presents four possible scenarios:

1. If you have low control and believe you have low control, you will probably experience stress.

2. If you have high control but believe you have low control, you will also probably experience stress.

3. If you have low control but believe you have high control, stress is probably not an issue. The real issue is possible mental illness.

4. If you have high control and believe you have high control, you will probably experience low stress.

Control and belief about control play a large part in workplace stress. The National Institute for Occupational Safety & Health (NIOSH) published a report in 1999 identifying what it believed to be the most significant stressors in the workplace for employees.[3] Virtually all of them were predicated on the belief that employees had no control to change these stressors, such as heavy workloads, boring work, lack of participation in making decisions, and having to work in uncomfortable conditions. The study, however, did not take individual differences into account, such as how certain employees might simply accept their work conditions (either in grudging silence or complaining to coworkers, family, or friends), while others might take steps to seek change in the conditions they disliked, by either making changes on their own or seeking assistance or support from management.

Situational Competence

While *control* relates to your freedom or opportunity to make changes to a negative event or situation, *competence* refers to your ability to do so, or your perception of your ability to do so.

Situational competence refers to your ability to handle specific problems. That is, although you may feel competent to handle life in general and most of what it throws at you, you probably have some specific areas where you feel helpless.

However, competence can also be a function of your personality in general and therefore is covered in the "General Life Competence" section later in this chapter.

Usually, situational competence is a function of experience. For example, if you are driving, get a flat tire, and have changed dozens of flats in your lifetime, the situation may not be very stressful. However, if you don't even know what a lug nut is or how to use a jack, get ready for some stress.

Or suppose you wake up in the middle of the night to find a burst pipe spewing water in the bathroom, you will probably experience quite a bit of stress if you don't know anything about the main shutoff valve. If you're a plumber, though, the only stress you'll experience will relate to having to wipe up the already spilled water. You know how to deal with the rest.

I don't mind admitting that automobile breakdowns are my most serious area of situational incompetence. Prior to 1973 (the year I experienced my first automotive breakdown), I thought nothing of driving anywhere, at any time, in any weather conditions, whether it be five miles away or one thousand miles away.

On a snowy, windy, Sunday afternoon in January 1973, however, I was driving from my college town to my student teaching job in a community about forty miles away. About halfway there, the needle on the temperature gauge began rising, and rising, and rising, until my car began sputtering. I pulled over and stopped. At the time, I knew absolutely nothing about cars—what made them run, and what made them break down. All I knew was that I was two miles from the next town (population about 500), that there were no gas stations open, that it was cold and snowy, that it was quickly getting dark, and that my college roommates were out of town on break, so I had no one to call and no other source of transportation available.

To make a long story short, I hiked the two miles into the town, knocked on the door of the first house I saw, and explained my plight. The woman said she thought a couple of guys on the west end of town knew something about cars. After getting directions, I located the father-and-son team, who agreed to tow me to their homemade garage. They discovered a radiator leak but didn't have the material to patch it. They refilled the radiator with water, I gave them ten dollars for their trouble, and I headed on my way again with their warning echoing in my mind: "We don't know how long it will take for the water to leak out again, so you may get stranded again." Not a promising scenario, especially since I knew for a fact there were no other gas stations open between where I was and where I was headed that Sunday night.

I did make it safely, but the following weekend I experienced more problems on the way back home related to the thermostat, stranding me in another small town of about 700, where I spent the weekend awaiting car repairs. Since that time, I have always been skittish about driving very far from home.

As with control, competence depends on actual and perceived competence. Again, there are four possible scenarios:

1. If you have low competence and believe you have low competence, you will probably experience stress.

2. If you have high competence but believe you have low competence, you will also probably experience stress.

3. If you have low competence but believe you have high competence, again, stress is probably not an issue. The real issue may be mental illness.

4. If you have high competence and believe you have high competence, you will probably experience low stress.

Situational Stress: An Example

Let's take an example related to time pressure and see how these seven factors will determine your stress level:

1. *Knowledge.* If you have to get a report done by the end of the day but you think it's not due for another week, you will not experience time-related stress—at least not today. (You may when you find out tomorrow that your report is late.)

2. *Responsibility.* If you are involved in a project team that must file a report by the end of the day, your level of stress will depend in part on how much responsibility you have. If you're the project team leader, you may experience a lot of stress. If you're a temporary member whose role has been to offer consulting advice to the full-time team, you may not experience stress.

3. *Conscientiousness.* If you are expected to make twenty calls in two hours to gather information from people for a report due in your boss's office, you will "race against the clock" to reach these people if you are conscientious. You will grill the secretaries who answer the phones, ask for your

contact people's cell phone numbers, make a passionate plea that these people call you back, and probably place second calls to them if they don't return your calls within the allotted time.

4. *Caring and Value.* If you have to file a report by the end of the day and your job promotion (or job) depends on it, you may experience stress. If an employee in another department has to file a report for the same reason, you may experience no stress at all.

5. *Enjoyment.* If you have to file a report by the end of the day on a topic you absolutely detest and have been having great difficulty finding information on, you will likely experience significant stress. On the other hand, if the report is on a topic about which you are passionate, you may experience some stress, but the positive anticipation of working on the report will likely outweigh the stress.

6. *Control.* Let's say you have to file a report by the end of the day. However, one of the sources of information you need is a person whom you have been unable to contact. Furthermore, no one else is available to help you with the report. Result: stress. However, let's say that you have all of the information you need on hand. Furthermore, as a manager, you have the authority to delegate portions of the report to subordinates. Result: much less stress.

7. *Situational Competence.* You have to file a report by the end of the day. You've been filing the same type of report for ten years. Stress level: probably nil. However, let's say this is the first time you've ever had to file a report, and let's also say that researching, organizing, and writing are not your strong suits. Result: major stress.

Assessment of Yourself

Beyond the seven factors that help you assess the situation, there are seven factors that relate to how you assess yourself.

General Life Competence

As noted earlier, situational competence refers to your ability to handle specific problems, usually based on past experience with those situations. However, experience isn't the only factor in determining competence-related stress. Overall self-esteem and self-confidence are important. People who have confidence in their abilities to handle life's situations in general tend to be less stressed when faced with negative events and situations, even if it is the first time they've faced them. People with low self-esteem and self-confidence, on the other hand, will likely experience stress in such situations, feeling they are not competent to handle things.

A second element to general life competence is the faith you have in yourself to make good decisions. That is, in assessing a situation, you may decide that you have the personal competence to handle it. However, if you decide that you don't have the competence, then the issue becomes whether you have the competence to turn the problem over to someone who is competent to solve the problem. For example, someone runs into the side of your garage, and it is about to collapse. Do you know how to find a contractor who can repair the problem quickly before the structure collapses and causes more damage, who is competent to do the job properly, and who is honest in terms of not overcharging you?

Active Courage

This relates to your propensity for taking risks. Each person has a specific tolerance for taking risks, but this can vary from life segment to life segment. For example, there are physical risk takers who enjoy nothing more than spending their weekends windsurfing, skydiving, or climbing mountains. Yet, they would be scared to death to quit their jobs and become self-employed. Others cringe at physical risk taking but are quite willing to take financial risks. Others like to experience risk in terms of committing crimes, such as robbery or drug dealing.

In one of Roseanne's (then known as Roseanne Barr) early stand-up routines on *The Tonight Show*, she poked fun at physical risk takers: "Hey, you want to really live on the edge? Get married, get a job, have kids, and stare a thirty-year mortgage in the face, you skydiving wimp!"

The message here: The level of stress you experience in a particular situation will be determined in part by how much of a risk taker you are in life in general and in the specific situation you're facing.

Passive Courage

While active courage relates to your willingness to create or voluntarily enter situations that have the potential to cause stress (risk creation), passive courage relates to how much courage you have to face situations that happen on their own and of which you find yourself a part, whether you like it or not (risk acceptance). Example: A tornado is heading your way. How well can you deal with that reality?

In terms of passive courage, you can experience stress if you suffer from the inability to be flexible enough to deal with the uncertainty or unpredictability of a situation. For some people, uncertainty and unpredictability lead to feelings of fear, futility, and helplessness. For others, such situations may be seen simply as challenges that they can use to test their mettle.

Flexibility

Flexibility as defined here relates to how much you feel you need to control a situation. This is different from the concept of control discussed earlier, which relates to how much control you are free to exert over a situation. Flexibility relates to how much control you insist on exerting. That is, if you like to micromanage situations and feel very uncomfortable when everything is not just perfect at all times, then you will probably view any minor detour from perfection with stress.

For example, if you are a strict disciplinarian with your children, expect them to be perfect angels "24–7," allow then no freedom, have numerous tasks for them to perform, and demand that these tasks be done to perfection at specified times, then you can expect to be stressed quite often—when your children turn out to be what they are—children.

Humor

The extent to which you feel stress in a situation can also be determined to a degree by how humorous an attitude you have toward life in general, or how much humor you can find in specific negative or potentially negative situations. Joel Goodman, director of the HUMOR Project (Saratoga Springs, New York), who presents seminars on humor nationwide, and whom I have interviewed for numerous articles on the value of humor in the workplace, suggests that one ability of humor is to help people reframe the experience of situations that they might otherwise find stressful.[4]

One example of the value of humor occurred in the 1972 movie *What's Up, Doc?* with Barbra Streisand and Ryan O'Neal. Near the end of the movie, which takes place in San Francisco, there is an extended car chase scene with about a dozen people in a half dozen cars. One of the carless participants flags down a car driven by a tourist from England and directs him to get involved in the chase. While everyone else is stressed out "to the max" for reasons of his or her own, as well as because of the danger of driving at high speeds up and down the hills of San Francisco (and down a flight of stairs!), the English gentleman is roaring with laughter, thoroughly enjoying the unexpected excitement of being able to participate in a ten-minute car chase and add some enjoyment to his life.

Optimism

One of the most important books ever written about the human condition, in my opinion, is Dr. Martin Seligman's *Learned Optimism*.[5] Seligman's research over twenty years has shown that how people look at specific situations determines whether they are optimists or pessimists, and that pessimism can lead to helplessness in life, which can ultimately lead to lifelong hopelessness.

Seligman identifies three constructs that determine optimism or pessimism, based on how you respond to specific situations:

1. *Personalization.* When something bad happens, a pessimist internalizes (blames himself for the situation), whereas an optimist externalizes (blames circumstances beyond his control). When something good happens, a pessimist externalizes (gives credit to the situation itself), whereas an optimist internalizes (gives himself credit for the situation).

2. *Permanence.* When something bad happens, a pessimist assumes the situation will remain permanent, whereas an optimist assumes the situation will be temporary. When something good happens, a pessimist assumes the situation will be temporary, whereas an optimist assumes the situation will remain permanent.

3. *Pervasiveness.* When something bad happens, a pessimist assumes that the negative experience will begin to pervade all aspects of his life (that everything else will go bad), whereas an optimist assumes that the negative experience will remain isolated to that one part of his life and everything else will continue to be positive. When something good happens, a pessimist assumes it will be limited to that one area of his life, whereas an optimist assumes it will expand to all other areas of his life.

In sum, the "learned optimist" is someone who explains good events as permanent, pervasive, and caused internally; bad events are explained as temporary, limited in scope, and externally caused.

Seligman notes that a person's permanence and pervasiveness scores determine his "Hope" score, which is the most important score in determining helplessness and hopelessness.

"Learned pessimism" (the distress-prone personality) leads to "learned helplessness," which is defined as the tendency to give up on problems or negative situations prematurely due to feelings of inability to control life's situations. Learned helplessness ultimately leads to "learned hopelessness," the tendency to collapse under pressure or during negative situations. This is a life that ends up being characterized by frequent or chronic stress, anxiety, and depression.

Beyond the negative mental and emotional results of learned helplessness, one study found that women who scored high on learned helplessness had a greater risk of contracting cancer.[6] In addition, numerous studies have shown that centenarians are those who are able to shake off even major devastations in life due to a pervasive spirit of optimism about life in general.[7]

Hardiness

Another term for hardiness is *resilience*. Hardy, resilient people are those who have a strong tolerance for situations that might be defined as stressful. That is, they tend not to get stressed as much as other people might, and if they do get stressed, they tend to bounce back quickly.

In addition, hardy, resilient people have a wider range of stress tolerance than most people. That is, some people prefer to live in the high-stress zone (overload), such as engaging in extreme sports. These are people who might experience stress in boring situations (underload). Others tend to prefer living in the underload zone, because they know they get very stressed in overload situations. Still others prefer a narrow middle ground, with little excitement and little boredom. Hardy, resilient people are those who tend to be relatively comfortable in all three areas of the spectrum—underload when it occurs, midrange when it occurs, and overload when it occurs. They make the most of each situation as it occurs.

Furthermore, although less-resilient people tend to see potentially stressful situations as "terrible," "outside of their influence," and "disruptive to security," resilient people tend to see these situations as "interesting," "able to be influenced," and "challenging" (good for growth).

Another hallmark of resilient people: They usually become stronger when the pressure increases. A metaphor for strength during times of pressure relates to liquid mercury, which exerts stronger and stronger opposing pressure as more pressure is placed on it. I had the opportunity to experience this firsthand in the early 1960s when we lived in Canada and visited a gold mine in northern Ontario, where my father knew the mine manager. During the gold-mining process, miners encounter liquid mercury, which is brought up in large buckets. The manager had me make a fist and force it down into the bucket. I was able to push my fist down into the cold liquid for three or four inches, but after that, the pressure became stronger. Using all of my strength (not much, admittedly, for a young, skinny teenager), I was able to sink it another two inches, but no farther. I was still at least four inches from the bottom of the bucket. Even the strongest miner there, the manager assured me, was unable to push his fist all the way to the bottom because of the opposing pressure.

So it is with the most hardy, resilient people. The stronger the opposition becomes, the stronger they become. Take the example of President George W. Bush. Dismissed as a lightweight by most of the nation during the presidential campaign and in his first few months as president, he has shown tremendous resilience and hardiness since September 11, becoming much better than anyone ever expected he was capable of being. Prior to 9/11, many thought he was a brainless goof-off who did nothing but stumble over his own words. Since then, he has held the nation together, rebuilt confidence, orchestrated the ouster of the Afghan government, created a Homeland Security Department, shown no fear or wavering, and maintained a consistent war on terrorism.

Summary

In this chapter, you learned that the perceptions you have of situations that can be considered stressful are often largely based on your personality. There are seven factors that are based on your assessment of the situation. These are knowledge, responsibility, conscientiousness, caring and value, enjoyment, control, and situational competence. There are also seven factors that are based on your assessment of yourself. These are general life competence, active courage, passive courage, flexibility, humor, optimism, and hardiness.

PART II

Basic Stress-Prevention Strategies

Part I was designed to help you become aware of the significant damage that stress can cause in your life; understand the categories, causes, and perceptions of stress; and understand the "stress personality"—characteristics unique to you that will determine whether you experience stress in specific situations.

Part II will look at a number of different ways to begin to gain control of stress in your life and ultimately begin to eliminate it completely.

Chapter 4 covers the very important role of maintaining your physical health through sleep, nutrition, exercise, and relaxation.

Chapter 5 will take the fourteen personality traits introduced in Chapter 3 and show you ways to begin to shift them so that experiences that once caused you stress will no longer do so.

Finally, Chapter 6 will cover a number of individual steps

you can consider to help cope with stress. One is understanding how introverts and extroverts respond to stress. Others include a number of additional steps to prevent stress, respond to stress, and decompress from stress that continues to occur.

CHAPTER FOUR

Stress and Health

When it comes to alleviating stress in your life, in terms of both preventing it from occurring in the first place and recovering from it when it does occur, the most important step you can take is to keep yourself healthy. In specific, this involves four main areas: sleep, nutrition, exercise, and relaxation.

Sleep

For better or worse, the link between stress and sleep is a vicious cycle. Research conducted by the National Sleep Foundation found the most common negative mental effect of lack of sleep is the inability to handle stressful situations (reported by 63 percent of respondents).[1] However, research by the same organization also found that, by far, the most common *cause* of the inability to sleep is stress (reported by 46 percent as the number one cause). In second place were medical problems (reported by only 7 percent). In sum, lack of sleep increases stress, and the stress then interferes with the ability to sleep.

Adding to the problem is the fact that a lot of people find themselves staying up late watching TV to try to decompress from stress. However, new research definitively shows that they would be much better off spending that time sleeping. Over a hundred years ago, prior to the invention of the lightbulb, people slept an average of ten hours a night. Today, the average is between six and seven hours, with fully one-third of the adult population trying to survive on six hours or less. However, medical research shows that almost everyone needs eight hours. Although there are some individual differences, there are not as many as most people think. For example, a lot of people report with pride that they can "get by" with six hours of sleep. However, there is a big difference between "getting by" and functioning at your best. It was not until 1996 that the American Medical Association began to recognize sleep medicine as a specialty area. Even sleep researchers are now just beginning to fully comprehend the mysteries of sleep and its powerful consequences for the quality of life.

One of these consequences is the ability to cope with stress. When you consistently get a full night's sleep, you can operate "on all eight cylinders" and can usually cope with most situations that would otherwise cause you stress. However, if you are sleep deprived, your energy levels and coping abilities suffer. Thus, situations that would not otherwise cause you to experience stress can lead to stress, because you don't have the physical, mental, and emotional energy to deal with them properly.

The results of a six-year study of sleep habits showed that mortality rates of people sleeping less than six hours a night were 2.5 times greater than those sleeping seven to eight hours.[2] One reason: Sufficient sleep helps reduce levels of cortisol in the blood, which, as discussed in Chapter 1, is associated with chronic stress. The study also found that sleep-deprived people average twice as many visits to the doctor a year than do people who are not sleep deprived. They also have twice as many infections, because their immune systems are weakened.

There can be two reasons for failure to get enough sleep. One is simply choosing to stay up later than you should or get up earlier than you should. That is, today's fast-paced life may encourage you to skimp on your sleep. You may feel obligated to "burn the candle at both ends" to meet your responsibilities to your job, your children, your housework, and yourself. An even more pervasive culprit is the lure of technology, such as late-night television, videos, and Internet surfing. Resist these temptations. Realize that the greatest favor you can do for yourself and everyone else in your life is to have your head on a pillow "sawing logs" for at least eight hours every night.

The second reason for sleep deprivation is not an unwillingness to get enough sleep, but an inability to do so (insomnia). Here is a list of things that can help you get better sleep:

- Be sure your mattress, pillow, and bed sheets are comfortable.

- Keep your bedroom dark and cool. Consider a white-noise generator, such as an empty vaporizer, to mask unwanted noises.

- Exercise during the day. This can help produce a restful night's sleep, because the exercise helps to alleviate stress.

- Make sure any medications you take before bed do not act as stimulants. If so, check with your physician about taking different medications or taking them at different times of day.

- Stay away from caffeine and nicotine before bed. For some people, caffeine can even have an effect sixteen hours later, so even coffee in the morning can cause insomnia. Chocolate cake for dessert after supper can have the same effect.

▶ Avoid alcohol. Although it is a depressant, it wears off after three or four hours and can cause you to awaken at night and not be able to fall back asleep.

▶ Eat a light snack before bed, since hunger can awaken you. For example, tuna, dark-meat turkey, and bananas have chemicals that induce sleep. Warm milk or herbal tea can also help relax you. However, stay away from large, heavy meals before bed, especially those that contain fats and spices, since the digestion process can keep you awake.

▶ Try taking a warm bath or shower to help relax you before bed.

▶ If you want entertainment, read a book just before bed. Stay away from TV and computer screens. The flicker of the line rasters affects the brain and can keep you awake for an hour or two.

▶ Stop doing everything at least thirty minutes before bed. Use that time to sit quietly in a chair and relax. Take notes if you want. Then, put everything out of your mind before you go to bed.

▶ If you still have a tendency to worry and "mind race" after you get into bed, keep a tape recorder or a flashlight and note card by your bed so you can record thoughts as they occur and not worry about forgetting them.

▶ Consider certain vitamins and minerals that help promote relaxation before bed, such as calcium, magnesium, and some of the B vitamins. However, check with your physician before taking these, as they can have some negative side effects. Excess calcium can clog the carotid arteries. Excess levels of some B vitamins can lead to irreversible nerve and muscle damage.

▶ Consider some herbs that have relaxing properties, including passionflower, valerian, hops, and skullcap. Again, though, check with your physician first.

▶ What about melatonin? Once hailed as the "breakthrough natural sleep aid," and also a cancer preventer to boot, recent research suggests that it may actually promote cancer growth in certain individuals. Again, check with your physician first.

▶ As a last resort, consider over-the-counter sleeping pills or prescription sleeping pills, but be warned there can be a number of unhealthy side effects.

Nutrition

Nutrition affects how well we can cope with the physical and mental demands of stress:

▶ Good nutrition prepares us to cope with stress by providing nutrients we need to fight off stress.

▶ Poor nutrition creates stress by mimicking the physical effects of stress.

▶ Stress can ruin a healthy diet by depleting certain nutrients and increasing our need to replace them.

What to Stop Ingesting

When stress occurs, the body, assuming that the stress is temporary and that it needs to bolster its ability to cope with the stress, does an interesting thing: It begins craving the very things that maintain the effects of the stress reaction. That is, the body seeks substances that reduce its ability to alleviate stress! These five substances are nicotine, caffeine, alcohol, refined sugar and white flour, and salt.

Nicotine (Smoking) In the short term, nicotine stimulates the endocrine system, mimicking the biochemical effects of stress, such as increased blood pressure and pulse, and the secretion of adrenaline (which prepares the body for short-term stress). Also, being a stimulant, it can cause insomnia, which prevents sleep (as discussed earlier). Third, nicotine also increases cortisol, which is released during chronic stress.

Over the long term, smoking promotes hypertension, cardiovascular disease, respiratory illnesses, stroke, and an impaired immune system (reduced resistance to infections and cancer). All of these are also long-term effects of stress.

Caffeine Like nicotine, caffeine also stimulates the endocrine system, mimicking the biochemical effects of stress, such as increased blood pressure and pulse, and secretion of adrenaline (which prepares the body for short-term stress). The reason: Caffeine is a chemical belonging to the xanthine group of drugs, which are powerful amphetamine-like substances that increase metabolism.

Also, like nicotine, caffeine is a stimulant, which can cause insomnia, which prevents sleep (as discussed earlier). Caffeine is also a diuretic that causes excess urinary excretion of B vitamins and vitamin C, both important for stress resilience. In sum, stay away from caffeine as much as possible. This includes coffee, iced tea, many soft drinks, and chocolate.

Alcohol Alcohol, as it is absorbed into the body, requires a steady supply of B vitamins, particularly thiamin, niacin, and folic acid, which it then excretes. As discussed later, these B vitamins are powerful stress resisters. In addition, alcohol excretes four essential stress-prevention minerals: magnesium, calcium, potassium, and zinc. Finally, alcohol acts as a diuretic, causing the body to lose water. As this dehydration occurs, the body experiences this as a stressor, resulting in additional increased levels of cortisol.

Refined Sugar and White Flour If stress encourages you to reach for donuts, cakes, cookies, pies, soft drinks, and candy, resist the temptation. Again, these substances actually facilitate increased stress, because they deplete B-complex vitamins, which are vital to stress reduction. A high-sugar diet can also lead to hypoglycemia (low blood sugar). Symptoms of hypoglycemia can mimic those of stress, such as trembling and increased cardiac activity.

Salt This is the mineral most responsible for regulating the body's water balance. Excess salt leads to water retention, which can increase nervous tension and blood pressure. The body needs only one gram of salt per day, but most people get four to eight. The most common and abundant sources of salt are table salt; crackers; pretzels; potato chips; and most processed foods, such as many TV dinners. Many boxed rices are also high in sodium. The real "killer" though? Soy sauce, which can contain over 1,000 milligrams of sodium per serving.

Consider switching from salt to potassium (sold in most supermarkets near where the salt is sold). Common words on the label may be *no salt* or *salt substitute*. Refer to information on the back, though, to make sure that the product is, indeed, potassium. However, check with your doctor first to make sure he or she feels it is safe for you to reduce your salt intake and increase your potassium intake.

What to Start Ingesting

Overall, a healthy diet keeps you mentally alert and physically healthy, making it easier to cope successfully with situations that might otherwise cause stress. Good nutrition supports the adrenal glands, which play a critical role in the stress response. Stress causes the adrenals to shrink, but a healthy diet counteracts this, helping to maintain adrenal gland health.

A healthy diet consists of:

▶ Whole grains and high-fiber breads, cereals, rice, and pasta

▶ Legumes (beans, etc.)

▶ Fruits and vegetables (preferably fresh)

▶ Moderate amounts of lean protein and/or soy

▶ Nonfat or low-fat dairy products

▶ Fish

▶ Healthy fats from nuts, seeds, and their oils

In addition, there are the vitamins, minerals, and other supplements you need in order to combat stress:

▶ B vitamins, especially B1 (thiamin), B2 (riboflavin), B3 (niacin), B5 (pantothenic acid), and B6 (pyridoxine).

▶ Vitamin C.

▶ The "electrolyte soup" minerals:

  ▶ Calcium balanced with magnesium.

  ▶ Sodium balanced with potassium. In general, to maintain this balance, reduce your sodium intake and increase your potassium intake (as detailed earlier). The reason: The average diet contains one unit of potassium for every two units of sodium but should contain one unit of sodium for every five units of potassium (ten times higher than what it is).

▶ Selenium.

▶ Zinc.

▶ Omega-3 fatty acids (which are abundant in DHA and EPA fish oils).

There are two ways to get these nutrients—food sources and bottled supplements. Each has advantages and disadvantages.

Food Sources

▶ B vitamins from most cold cereals, whole grains, pork, peanut butter, poultry, beef liver, milk, and yogurt

▶ Vitamin C from orange juice, bell peppers, broccoli, and strawberries

▶ Potassium from most fruits/vegetables (especially apples, carrots, bananas, oranges, potatoes, and tomatoes)

▶ Calcium from milk and dark green vegetables

▶ Magnesium from grains, nuts, and leafy green vegetables

▶ Selenium from whole grains, tuna, Brazil nuts, and garlic

▶ Zinc from beef, wheat bran, and nuts

▶ Omega-3 fatty acids from salmon, albacore (white) tuna, bluefin tuna, and mackerel

The upside of getting these nutrients from food is that the sources are natural, there is little risk of overdosing, and you benefit from the natural fiber in the foods. The downside is that to get as much of these nutrients as is necessary to effectively reduce or eliminate the physiological stress response, you may have to ingest pounds and gallons of these foods each day.

Bottled Supplements The upside of taking bottled vitamins, minerals, and other supplements is that you can accurately measure how much you are getting of each nutrient. The recommended daily allowances (RDAs), which were established in the 1940s, were designed to prevent deficiencies such as scurvy (lack of vitamin C), pellagra (lack of niacin), beriberi (lack of vitamin B1), etc. The ideal amounts (the amounts needed to maintain strong, robust health), though, are much greater than the RDAs. Again, you'd have to ingest large quantities of food and drink to achieve these ideal levels. In addition, one of the most important minerals, selenium, which was once prevalent in crop-growing soils, has virtually been depleted in the last thirty years, meaning that foods contain very little of this vital mineral anymore.

On the downside, bottled vitamins, minerals, and other supplements are unregulated by the Food and Drug Administration. Although one potential result is contaminated batches, a more common problem is people taking excessive amounts of these substances (to the point of toxicity), which can lead to significant negative side effects and health risks—including death. Excess amounts of vitamin B6, for example, can cause permanent muscle tissue and nerve damage. Excess amounts of calcium can clog carotid arteries.

If you seek these nutrients from bottled supplements, rather than directly from food sources, check with your physician first, unless the only supplement you take is a nationally recognized brand of multivitamin, such as One-A-Day or Centrum. In fact, the very best advice related to stress-reducing nutrition is to eat a healthy, well-balanced diet (all the stuff you've been reading about for years in magazines), and supplement this with a nationally recognized brand of multivitamin. Again, stay away from additional supplements unless you consult with your physician first.

Finally, if you do begin taking supplements, it is important to do so consistently and to realize that it can take a month or more before the gradual physiological effects begin to take place in your body and a noticeable reduction in stress occurs. These nutrients work slowly and naturally with the body, unlike prescription medications, which quickly invade the body and upset its natural balance.

What about herbal supplements? Certain herbs can help provide calming effects, such as skullcap, valerian, hops, and passionflower. However, these are not recommended on a regular basis, since herbs are not a natural part of a normal diet, unlike vitamins, minerals, and certain other supplements, which occur naturally in food. In fact, stress-reducing herbs act much like pharmaceuticals and alcohol, in that they simply mask stress symptoms, rather than strengthen the body naturally to prepare to cope with stress, as vitamins and minerals do.

Exercise

There has been enough written in recent years about the many benefits of exercise, including how it reduces stress before and after the fact. As such, we won't go into a lot of detail here, other than a few specifics:

- One study found that nonexercisers had more depression, stress, and stress-circulating hormones than exercisers.[3]

- Another study found that fit students had lower pulse rates than nonfit students when taking mildly stressful word memory tests.[4]

▶ A third study found that when asked to solve a set of unsolvable problems, all students experienced muscular tension, but fit students showed less muscular tension and no increase in blood pressure, while nonfit students had more tension and increased blood pressure.[5]

Exercise reduces stress by:

▶ Reducing adrenal gland secretions of adrenaline and nor-adrenaline

▶ Decreasing cortisol

▶ Decreasing cholesterol and reducing blood pressure

▶ Increasing brain endorphins (which elevate mood)

▶ Enhancing the immune function by bathing cells in toxic by-products associated with energy expenditure (which gives your immune system a workout, making it more robust)

Although nonaerobic workouts (such as weight lifting and push-ups) are useful, aerobic exercise is better for stress-management purposes. This includes walking, running, calisthenics, walking up and down stairs, and riding an exercise bike, etc.

If you really want to make giant strides in getting started on an exercise program, consider one that will not only get you physically fit but also save you a ton of money. Mow your lawn with a push mower! Instead of spending $1,000 for a treadmill and another $2,000 for a riding mower, spend $200 for a push mower. It will provide an exceptionally good (and cheap) workout.

Relaxation

There are several options here: meditation, breathing, and body relaxation.

Meditation

Meditation is a very important component of stress prevention. It is discussed in detail in Chapter 8. Meditation generates the opposite effect of stress. Whereas stress triggers biochemical responses, meditation triggers the opposite responses: lower blood pressure, reduced muscle tension, decreased heart rate, and slower breathing.

In addition, meditation helps the body retain stores of a vital age-prevention hormone called DHEA. Whenever the body feels stress, it depletes its store of DHEA, and as we age, our bodies are able to produce less and less of this important hormone. Meditation, again, protects our supplies of DHEA, thus slowing down the aging process. One study showed that male meditaters had 23 percent more DHEA than male nonmeditaters, and female meditaters had 47 percent more DHEA than female nonmeditaters.[6]

Meditation is even good for oral health! One study linking the effects of stress to tooth decay found that after twenty minutes of meditation, subjects had lower levels of plaque-forming bacteria in their mouths.[7] At the same time, their salivary glands produced saliva with high levels of calcium, phosphorus, and fluoride, all of which help protect tooth enamel.

Breathing

Stressed breathing is short and shallow. Relaxed breathing is long and deep. There is even a theory that one of the determinants of life span is the number of breaths we take. That is, we are preprogrammed for a certain number of breaths in life. If we use these up in our early years with fast, short, shallow breathing, we may die younger than people who are in the habit of breathing slower, longer, and deeper.

The best approach is to develop a habit of taking slow, long, and deep breaths all the time. Until you can create this habit, though, take the time to practice this type of breathing two or three times a day for a few minutes. One tip many experts recommend is to make your exhalations twice as long as your inhalations.

Body Relaxation

One effective method of body relaxation is to utilize a three-step process: Relax your mind. Relax your breathing. Relax your body. Here is the theory:

- When you relax your mind, you can relax your lungs.

- When you relax your lungs, you can breathe properly.

- When you breathe properly, you can slow down your heartbeat.

- When you slow down your heartbeat, you can relax your mind more.

- When you relax your mind more, you can breathe more slowly.

- When you breathe more slowly, your heart slows further.

- And so on, and so on.

Relax your mind. Bring all of your thoughts from the outside world to your body, focusing on the area of the brain behind your forehead. Then regulate your concentrated mind until it is relaxed. Do this by letting your thoughts be calm and peaceful. Disregard surrounding distractions. Focus on your body. Relax your concentrated mind. Although your mind may be clear, it may be tense from concentration, so learn to concentrate without mental tension. To do this, focus on something else, like your breathing, the sensation of your lungs expanding and contracting. As you exhale, feel your body relax to a deeper level.

Relax your breathing. As you relax your mind, you will be able to relax your breathing. Your breathing is closely related to your thoughts and feelings. Once your mind is calm, breathing can be independent of thought. First, neutralize the effects of your emotions on your breathing. Second, realize that breathing is caused by the physical motion of the body, so relax all the muscles that relate to breathing. Feel the muscles of your diaphragm moving. As you do this, you will feel your chest and solar plexus loosening up. When your chest is loose, you have achieved a fundamental relaxation state.

Relax your body. Relaxing your body is the first step to regulating your body. Only when you are relaxed are you able to sense your body's root, center, balance, and regulation. Sense the muscles in your body. Once your mind can reach these muscles, it will be led to the organs to sense and relax them.

One study showed that malignant melanoma patients who learned and practiced relaxation techniques were three times less likely to die than those who did not.[8]

Summary

In this chapter, you learned that there are several things you can do to begin to reduce the stress response in your life. These in-

volve the four most important basic health improvement strategies: getting enough sleep, eating properly (giving up substances
that promote stress and replacing them with substances that reduce stress), exercising in ways that reduce stress and begin to
build resilience to stress, and finding ways to relax to both alleviate stress and help prevent it from recurring.

CHAPTER FIVE

Rebuilding Attitudes and Perceptions

In Chapter 3 I suggested that there are fourteen different attitudes and perceptions that largely determine whether you will experience stress during a certain situation or event. The first seven related to your assessment of the situation itself. The remaining seven related to your assessment of yourself.

Here, we look at some steps you can take to modify these assessments and, in so doing, reduce the frequency and intensity of stress you feel in life. (Refer back to Chapter 3 if you would like a refresher on the details of the roots of these perceptions and attitudes.)

Changing Your Assessment of the Situation

Here are some ways to change the seven ways you may look at specific situations.

Knowledge

As noted earlier, "Ignorance is bliss" when it comes to stress. If you don't know that a situation is dangerous, you will not be stressed. In terms of making changes, I don't recommend becoming more ignorant or less knowledgeable. However, there are still a couple of steps you can take to reduce knowledge-related stress.

First, stay away from (or at least stop paying attention to) people who always seem to be talking about how terrible things are in the world, in the nation, or in your community. There are some people who just seem to revel in negativity, as though they have their own personal rain cloud above their heads. Five people can be sitting around talking about a situation in either positive or neutral terms, and all it takes is a sixth person to come along and share a horror story or some negative perception designed to bring everyone down.

Example: You're having a discussion about what a wonderful school district your town has, and Negative Nellie pipes up, "Oh, but they have a huge drug problem there! None of the kids are safe!" If you buy into this kind of negativity, you're going to feel stressed each and every day you send your kids to school. If you have a concern about such a comment, talk to some other people, especially teachers, administrators, board members, and other parents. They should be able to put the problem (if any) into perspective for you. Although there may indeed be kids in the school using drugs, you'll probably find out that it's not in the epidemic proportions suggested by Negative Nellie.

Second, if you find yourself glued to the television set every day watching the news, find some other way to pass the time. News networks earn their income by continually coming up with crisis situations designed to keep people watching. Frankly, 99 percent of it does not and never will have any direct effect on you. However, if you watch it all the time, you'll find yourself in a constant state of stress, worrying about "how the world is falling apart."

On a personal note, I didn't even own a television between the time I left home for college in 1969 and when I got married in 1980. In sum, I missed twelve years of "news." I later found out that people had been stressed every day during that time period about this or that crisis. I didn't know about any of them, and none of them affected me. In fact, it actually worked to my advantage. In late 1974, I asked for a very large raise from my boss and received it. It was only a decade or more later that I learned the nation had been in the throes of a major financial crisis in 1973 and 1974, with the economy in terrible shape and tens of thousands of people losing their jobs. Had I known about any of this, I probably would have been worried about my own job instead of asking for a raise.

The bottom line is that it is important to remember that certain individuals and the news media thrive on trying to make people miserable. Although you do need to take steps to become knowledgeable about real threats to your safety, don't get caught up in someone else's world of negativity.

Responsibility

If you find yourself getting stressed out frequently in life because you take on responsibility for issues that are not your responsibility, learn to let go and allow those who are responsible for them to handle them. You may want to make yourself available to these people if they need assistance, but insist that they take primary responsibility.

Conscientiousness

If you feel the weight of the world on your shoulders—that you are the person who has to handle everything and do so perfectly—ask yourself, "What will happen if I don't get this done? Or don't get it done on time? Or don't get it done perfectly?"

Realize that although conscientiousness can be an admirable quality that will get you far in life, too much of it will drive you crazy and ultimately be counterproductive. Look at situations realistically, decide what outcomes will have significant repercussions, focus on those, and devote less attention to some of the less significant ones.

Caring and Value

As noted earlier in the "Caring and Value" section in Chapter 3, the less you value and care about a situation, the less likely you are to experience stress. I don't recommend caring less about situations for which you should naturally care. What you can do is assess each situation and determine whether it is appropriate to care. Then, you can stop caring about situations where there is no need to do so and focus attention on those for which it is appropriate to care.

Enjoyment

As noted in the "Enjoyment" section in Chapter 3, the more you enjoy something, the less likely you are to be stressed by it. Can you *create* enjoyment? I don't recommend forcing yourself to like something that you don't naturally like. However, you can create a habit of being more open to experiences. Many people have closed minds, telling themselves that they don't like something without ever having spent enough time studying it to see if this is really the case. Often, by taking the time to explore a subject or experience with an open mind, you may find that you can at least shift from a "don't like" to a "neutral" attitude, or a "neutral" attitude to a "like" attitude.

For example, if you've always disliked the idea of learning about basic auto maintenance and repair, a little time reading a basic book on car care may change your mind to the point where you're willing to get involved with some basic care. As such, if and when your vehicle breaks down on you, you may be less stressed.

Control

This is one of the most important determinants of stress, and one of the most important determinants of life happiness in general. In fact, if you want to start an angry, intense, emotional, and volatile argument, find two people whose views of overall life control are at opposite ends of the spectrum (one person who feels "stuff happens" and that there is little anyone can do to control life's circumstances, the other who feels he can exert a lot of control over his life). The degree of control that you feel you have in life tends to be a basic, almost primitive, belief. It usually begins early in life as you watch and listen to your parents in relation to control issues. Religion plays a key role, too, with some religions preaching that we have little control, and others preaching that we can have a lot of it. As such, control can be a sensitive issue for people. If you're a person who feels you have little control in life and are not willing to challenge this belief, then let this one go and move on to the next topic. However, be aware that you will probably continue to have stress in life as it relates to control issues.

If you are someone who currently feels you have little control but are willing to challenge this attitude, then I recommend beginning in small steps. Experiment. Take chances. If you're in a situation where you feel you have no control, pretend that you do. Try something that you have never tried before. See what happens.

Example: Your job continues to stress you out. Yet, you have never sat down and talked about your concerns with anyone in management. Consider doing so, not in an attack or complaining mode, but rather a problem-solving, cooperative mode. The key: Approach your boss or other member of management exactly the same way you would want to be approached by an employee if you were the boss—with respect, dignity, sensitivity, and maturity. If you find that your boss really is unreasonable, then you have to deal with that reality, or find another job. However, you may be surprised to find that he or she is open to your ideas for improvement.

It also must be said that, regardless of how much control you believe you have in life, no one has total control. As such, part of dealing with issues of "control versus stress" is to realize when it makes sense just to let something go that you cannot control. At the same time you let go, though, realize that you can also let go of the stress, because the situation is out of your control. Let others who are in positions of responsibility and authority deal with these issues.

For example, as I was waiting for the ambulance to arrive after I broke my hip, one reason I felt calm was that I knew there was nothing I could do to help myself. I had to place myself in the hands of experts—EMTs, emergency room personnel, and eventually a surgeon. Since I had no reason to believe these people were incompetent, I felt comfortable placing my care in their hands. I let them do what they needed to do, and I did whatever they told me to do.

Situational Competence

As noted earlier in the "Situational Competence" section in Chapter 3, there are two kinds of competence. One relates to competence in specific situations. The other relates to general life competence, which is covered later.

In situation-specific competence, there are some things you can do to increase competence and thus reduce stress. One is to refer back to the "Enjoyment" section. In almost all cases, people tend to be competent in areas they naturally enjoy. They are less competent, or totally incompetent, in areas they dislike. As such, if you want to become more situation-competent, open your mind to these areas, so that you can find more enjoyment.

A previous example related to auto maintenance. Another one relates to home repair. If you've never hammered a nail, sawed a piece of wood, or drilled a hole, you may find that you actually enjoy the experience, or at least don't detest it as much as you thought you might. You may not end up competent enough to build a new house, but at least you will be able to make some minor repairs around the house that might otherwise cause stress.

Also keep in mind something else discussed earlier in the "Situational Competence" section in Chapter 3: Competence is a function of both actual competence and perceived competence. When you challenge yourself in a particular situation where you currently feel incompetent, you may find that you are at least a bit more competent than you think.

Example: I used to live next door to a single mother who purchased a ceiling fan/light combination. She came over one day very excited and insisted that I come over and see it. She thought about hiring an electrician to install it but was low on money, so she decided to try it herself. She read the instruction manual, got the tools, and did the job. She was quite proud of herself.

Changing Your Assessment of Yourself

As noted, there are several steps you can take to change your assessments of specific situations that might otherwise cause stress. There are also several steps you can take to change your assessment of yourself in general, so that you will not find so many situations or events to be stressful.

Although you will find that most of these steps are traditional, there is at least one step that you may find somewhat unusual. This step relates to *affirmations*. Affirmations are positive, pointed statements that you repeat to yourself on a regular basis. The idea is to inculcate the underlying beliefs reflected in the statements deep into your psyche. The result is to change existing negative or weak beliefs that you have into positive and strong beliefs.

There is a lot of argument over the use of affirmations. Naysayers generally cite one of two reasons why they are useless:

1. They don't work. This is disproved by the fact that millions of people have used them and continue to use them very successfully.

2. They are Pollyannish, promote the "rose-colored glasses" syndrome, and fail to reflect reality. My response to this claim is simple: If you fail to have a positive attitude toward something, it is because you have a negative attitude toward it. Why is a negative attitude any more real or right than a positive attitude? Your mind acts on the information it is being fed. If you and other people in your life have spent a lifetime feeding your mind with negative thoughts, why not spend the rest of your life replacing these with positive thoughts?

In sum, if you believe that affirmations can work, and if you repeat them with a spirit of genuine belief on a regular basis, you will find that your thinking will begin to change. When your thinking begins to change, your emotional reactions will begin to change. And when your emotional reactions begin to change, your behaviors will change.

With this introduction, let's look at some things you can do to make improvements in your assessments of yourself.

General Life Competence

Here, you can make improvements in three ways. The *first* improvement is to change your perception of your competence as it really exists. That is, if you really are more competent than you believe you are, you can discover this reality by challenging yourself to stand up to situations in which you may not feel competent. If and when you find that you are competent, your belief about your competence will eventually catch up to the reality of the situation—that you are competent in these specific situations.

One recommendation here is to be less of a perfectionist. If you believe that you must be 100 percent perfect at a task or challenge before you can consider yourself competent, yet you are only 90 percent competent, then find a way to feel comfortable with the 90 percent level of competence. A couple of good books on breaking the perfectionism habit are *Overcoming Perfectionism,* by Ann W. Smith, and *Too Perfect,* by Allan E. Mallinger and Jeannette Dewyse.

A second recommendation is to focus on the "now." What specific competence do you have to exhibit at this moment in order to be competent? Most people spend a lot of time thinking about possible problems in the future and worrying whether they will be competent to handle those problems if and when they occur. Most of the time, the problems don't occur. And even if they do, most people end up finding that they are more competent (resourceful) in handling the problem when it does arrive. Again, focus on the now. Trust that you will be competent enough when you need to be, so don't worry about it beforehand.

The *second* way to improve your general life competence is to become more competent in situations where you currently are not competent. One recommendation is to identify the situations in life that cause you the most frequent stress, but that do not seem insurmountable. These are the situations or events where you don't feel overwhelmed, but where you feel somewhat less than prepared to address. In other words, don't select an infrequent, major stressor. Select a minor stressor, and identify what specific competence you feel is lacking in your life to successfully deal with this situation. Then, find a way to learn about the competence and what you need to do to introduce it into your life.

Example: Have you ever plugged something into a socket and had a circuit blow? If you feel totally helpless and stressed in this situation, ask a friend, neighbor, or

> relative to explain the circuit breaker process to you, how to identify the tripped circuit, and how to reset it. If no one you know has any understanding of this process, then hire an electrician to explain it to you.

Over time, work through your list of stressors, identifying the missing competencies; determining what you need to learn, do, and/or practice to gain the competencies; and then doing so.

Of course, there will be certain situations where it is just not practical to learn the competency required to address a situation. This is where the *third* way to make an improvement in this area comes in. Gain some experience in finding skilled professionals to solve your problem. For example, although you may be able to gain some competencies in making minor vehicle repairs if your car becomes disabled while driving, you're not going to want to learn to rebuild an engine or transmission.

Identify all of the stressors in your life where you have no intention of becoming competent. Then spend time researching experts in these areas, people you have reason to believe are honest, competent, and caring. Then, keep the list handy for when you need them.

Some affirmations:

▶ *"I am competent. I make good decisions."*
▶ *"Security is handling things, not having things."*
▶ *"Whatever happens, I can handle it."*

Active Courage

There is debate over whether people can fundamentally change their personalities after a certain age (usually somewhere before ten or twelve), with the preponderance of the evidence being that although people can make some minor shifts, it is virtually impossible to become a radically different person (other than as a result of traumatic injury to the brain or chemical imbalances in the brain brought on by drug abuse or other foreign substances). One area of basic personality seems to be risk taking. That is, the evidence suggests that if you exhibit risk-taking personality characteristics early in life, you will likely retain these throughout your life. If you exhibit more cautious behavior, you will probably remain cautious throughout your life.

And, as noted earlier, those who tend to exhibit more risk-taking behaviors tend to be less negatively affected by situations that others might find stressful. That said, there are still some things you can do to expand your risk-taking behaviors.

First, if you find yourself exhibiting cautious behavior more often than you would like, it may be that you have more of a propensity for risk taking than you believe. That is, it may be that due to unfortunate circumstances over your lifetime when you have taken risks (either one or two major traumatic experiences or a series of minor negative experiences), you have placed the risk-taking portion of your personality in mothballs, not wanting to deal with such negative consequences anymore.

One way to run a reality check on just how much of a risk taker you are is to reflect on your childhood. Were you more of a risk taker then than now? Did you do things without fear that would send shivers up your spine now? Were you the adventurous sort? If so, then your current level of caution may be due to a buildup of fear based on problems you've encountered over the years as a result of risk-taking behavior. If this is the case, you may be able to identify these events yourself, sort things out, and once again embrace your risk-taking characteristics. If you are unable to do so on your own, then possibly some professional counseling could help.

Second, if you find that you have always been cautious in your life and you generally continue to feel comfortable with that characteristic, there may still be some things you can do to slightly increase your willingness to take risks—and thus ultimately experience less stress in your life.

The first place to look is health, specifically sleep, diet, exercise, and relaxation. As noted in Chapter 4, the most important key to dealing with stress is to be healthy, and adequate sleep, a healthy diet, regular exercise, and relaxation are the four most important elements. If your body becomes as healthy as possible, your mind will follow, and you will feel more alert, energetic, optimistic, and confident. The result: You will be more prone to engage in risk-taking behavior.

Third, begin experimenting, slowly, surely, and carefully at first. When you encounter a situation that was once just slightly beyond your willingness to take a risk, consider doing so. For example, if every time you are in a room full of people you get stressed and turn into a wallflower, take a small risk. Smile and say "hi" to someone—ideally the person who seems to be the least threatening.

Keep track of your "baby steps." Over time, you may find that you are able to take more and more risks—placing yourself in situations that you once found stressful and now find, if not invigorating, at least bearable.

It has been said that world travelers are comfortable wherever they are because they are continually expanding their comfort zones, which leads to some possible affirmations:

▶ *"I enjoy expanding my comfort zone."*
▶ *"I enjoy challenging situations."*

Passive Courage

Whereas expanding the active courage portion of your personality can be a real challenge, expanding the passive courage portion of your personality should be easier. The reason: To expand the active courage portion, you have to purposely step in front of risks. You have to make a conscious decision to do something. To expand the passive courage portion, however, all you have to do is decide not to step back or away from risks. You simply decide to do nothing. There are two scenarios to consider here—moderately risky scenarios and very risky scenarios.

1. When you find yourself in a moderately risky situation (one where your life or health is not at risk), simply hang around and see what happens. Just observe the situation. Realize that you are surviving.

Example: In Canada, part of the culture of growing up for some reason was engaging in fistfights—on and off the playground. During my formative years, I was in more than my share of them, sometimes winning, sometimes losing, more often than not reaching a draw. However, as I got older, I felt very uncomfortable anytime I was in a situation where people were physically accosting each other.

A few years ago, though, I realized I wanted to overcome this discomfort. I had my chance a couple of months later, when I was in a crowded nightclub one night, leaning up against the bar, and a fistfight broke out among three or four people a few feet away from me. Normally, I would have moved away from the melee as quickly as possible. This time, though, I had a different mind-set. I simply stood there and watched the fight ensue. I actually had a feeling of calm. One reason was that the fight didn't involve me, so there was a small chance I would end up in the middle of it. The other was that, having been involved in weight lifting, boxing, and tae kwon do for a couple of years, I felt confident that I could take care of myself if I did end up getting involved. A couple of participants ended up bouncing into me during the scuffle, but that was the extent of it. Bouncers broke it up within three or four minutes, and things went back to normal.

2. When you find yourself in a very risky situation, take appropriate steps to protect yourself, but do so calmly and rationally. Try to eliminate the fear and feelings of stress.

Example: If a tornado has been spotted and is possibly headed toward your home, don't panic. Simply take appropriate steps to protect yourself. In a home with a foundation, this means seeking shelter in a basement or small room on the far side of the tornado. In a mobile home, it means "Get the hell out of there!" Tornados, for some reason, love mobile homes!

Some affirmations:

▶ *"Safety is the presence of courage, not the absence of danger. I trust in my ability to survive."*

▶ *"I only need enough courage to face the current moment."*

▶ *"I will, after all, survive every moment but my last."*

Flexibility

Although it can be difficult to change your basic risk-taking nature (see the "Active Courage" section), shifting from rigidity to flexibility is something that virtually everyone should be able to do. The reason: Although we tend to be born with certain levels of risk-taking desire, flexibility is a basic human characteristic that is natural in everyone. It's just that, throughout life, as a way to protect ourselves from situations and circumstances in which we don't feel comfortable, some of us tend to become more rigid—more inflexible. Since flexibility is natural and rigidity is not, everyone should be able to become more flexible.

Again, start with the simple things. If you are a creature of habit, purposely break some habits once in a while, or allow others to break habits for you. For example, if you balance your checkbook every Saturday at noon, go out to lunch instead. If you eat supper out every Friday night at the same restaurant, eat somewhere else. If a friend interrupts your Sunday afternoon vacuuming ritual to see if you want to go shopping, do so. In sum, choose spontaneity over habit as often as is comfortable. Then do so even when it is slightly uncomfortable.

Eventually, as you begin to act more and more flexibly, you will begin to think more and more flexibly. When you begin to think more and more flexibly, you will be able to respond with much greater flexibility when otherwise stressful situations arise. In other words, rather than viewing these negative situations as stressful because they upset your natural order of things, you will simply view them as different, original, unique, or out of the ordinary, and you may actually find them interesting, rather than stressful.

Example: If the power goes out, a rigid person will fret about not being able to watch his favorite TV show or read a book. A flexible person, though, may gather his family around by candlelight and hold a family meeting to air grievances or to share recent interesting experiences—a really positive experience that would probably never have taken place otherwise.

"Yeah, but what about my TV show?" Don't worry. It will be rerun at least five or six times in the next two months. And even if it isn't, real life can be much more interesting and satisfying than Hollywood script life.

In researching his book *The Survivor Personality,* author Al Siebert found that the most resilient people were those who were also the most flexible in terms of being able to adopt different personality characteristics most appropriate for given situations. He defined this ability as "bi-phasic."[1]

Most personality tests ask if you are "playful or serious," "trusting or cautious," "intuitive or logical," "impulsive or stable," "easygoing or strong willed," etc. Bi-phasic people are those who answer "yes" to both, rather than to one or the other. In other words, they are "playful *and* serious," "trusting *and* cautious," "intuitive *and* logical," etc. It just depends on which characteristic is most appropriate and useful in the particular situation. For example, during a crisis at work or at home, they may be serious. But when things are going well, they know how to have a lot of fun. When dealing with most people, they may be very trusting, but when dealing with someone who makes them uncomfortable, they may be cautious. And so on.

Some affirmations to help you on your journey from rigidity to flexibility:

▶ *"I enjoy new situations."*

▶ *"I behave as appropriate for the situation."*

Humor

To pick up on some of the thoughts of Joel Goodman (mentioned in Chapter 3), a life with lots of humor tends to be a life with very little stress. This isn't to say that you should be callous (laughing at other people's misfortunes). It is to say that if you can take life and yourself a little more lightly, you will have a lot more fun and a lot less stress. One of Goodman's recommendations during workplace seminars on humor is to take your job seriously, but take yourself lightly. Be able to laugh at yourself.

Goodman also recommends creating your own "Humor First-Aid Kit" and keeping it handy. What makes you laugh? Examples of items can include a video of your favorite comedy show or movie, an audiocassette of your favorite comedian, a book by your favorite humorist, and toys or props for your desk. Without realizing it, I had been taking Goodman's advice for twenty years before I even interviewed him and heard about the idea. Every workday, Monday through Friday, for the last twenty years, I have taken thirty minutes for lunch, made a sandwich, and sat down to watch one of the sitcoms I've taped over the years: *The Three Stooges*, *The Jeffersons*, *All in the Family*, or *The Simpsons*. I find it hard to imagine how I'd get through the day if I didn't take this thirty-minute break for laughter.

Optimism

As noted in Chapter 3, Dr. Martin Seligman, in *Learned Optimism*, emphasizes that you have just as much right to become (or remain) an optimist as you to do become (or remain) a pessimist.

It really is just a choice—one you can make right here, right now.[2]

Again, let's look at the three constructs:

1. *Personalization.* When something bad happens, a pessimist internalizes (blames himself for the situation), whereas an optimist externalizes (blames circumstances beyond his control). When something good happens, a pessimist externalizes (gives credit to the situation itself), whereas an optimist internalizes (gives himself credit for the situation).

2. *Permanence.* When something bad happens, a pessimist assumes the situation will remain permanent, whereas an optimist assumes the situation will be temporary. When something good happens, a pessimist assumes the situation will be temporary, whereas an optimist assumes the situation will remain permanent.

3. *Pervasiveness.* When something bad happens, a pessimist assumes that the negative experience will begin to pervade all aspects of his life (that everything else will go bad), whereas an optimist assumes that the negative experience will remain isolated to that one part of his life and everything else will continue to be positive. When something good happens, a pessimist assumes it will be limited to that one area of his life, whereas an optimist assumes it will expand to all other areas of his life.

Keep problems in perspective. Compartmentalize.
In sum, to be an optimist:

▶ Begin to practice explaining good events as permanent, pervasive, and internally caused.

▶ Begin to practice explaining bad events as temporary, limited in scope, and externally caused.

Affirmations can be particularly helpful in your journey from pessimism to optimism:

▶ *"Everything that enters my life helps me in some way."*

▶ *"Every adversity has the seed of an equal or greater benefit."*

▶ *"What's good about this?"*

Hardiness

As noted in Chapter 3, another term for hardiness is resilience. Here is a stellar example of a woman who exhibits resilience, whom I interviewed for an article on stress a couple of years ago. One day in late 1997, Nancy Smith (not her real name), vice president of human resources for a shipyard, sat in her office assessing the situation. At the time, the painters' craft director and the business agent were sitting across from her arguing, wanting her to adjudicate their dispute. The owner of the company was on her cell phone, wanting to talk with her. The head of the production department was on her office phone, also wanting to talk to her. And, to top it off, the safety director and an employee were yelling at each other outside her office, waiting their turn to come in for some "dispute resolution."

In sum, everyone wanted immediate attention and an immediate solution to his or her problem. Although some people might lose it in such a situation, Smith responded calmly. To the two people arguing in her office, she said, "Please be quiet for now. I'll be with you in a moment." To the safety director and employee outside her office, she said, "Please come back in an hour if you haven't solved the problem on your own." To the production manager on her office phone, she said, "I'll call you back shortly." Then she got on her cell phone to find out what the president wanted.

At the time, Smith was putting in sixty to seventy hours a week at the shipyard. Most people would look at Smith and agree that she was resilient to stressful conditions in the workplace—and they would be right. However, there is something else about Smith that makes her resilience even more impressive. She has had multiple sclerosis for thirty-six years, and her neurologist can't believe she is still working at all. Hardly anyone with her degree of symptoms does any kind of work. Her explanation: disability, like stress, is only in your mind. She tells people that she doesn't consider herself disabled. Rather, she considers herself alternatively productive.

Some people have a relatively large stress zone (or range of stress tolerance), meaning they can be comfortable in situations that others might find boring and also in situations others might find too active, unstable, or risky. Others are more content at one end of the spectrum or the other, while still others are most comfortable in the middle.

One way to gain a wider zone of comfort is to build resilience. To do this, you first have to understand an important concept:

▶ *Protecting yourself from stress will not make you stronger or more resilient to stress.* Just as muscles atrophy when they are not exercised, your mind atrophies if it is not exposed to occasional stress.

▶ *To become resilient to stress, you must face stressful situations.* The key, though, is how you respond to the stress. The goal is to experience it in bite-sized chunks, in terms of both the intensity and duration of the experience. Then, proactively deal with the experience. Once you've done this, it is important to pull back and give yourself some recovery time. Then, expose yourself to more stress again.

Ideally, you should create your own stressful experiences, so that you can control both the intensity and duration. However, if you end up facing stressful situations not of your own doing, try to work through them as well as you can. Then, again, specifically set aside time to recover.

Take the example of weight lifting. Lifters build muscle and strength by purposely stressing their muscles. They achieve success this way:

▶ They don't lift too much weight the first time, so as not to rip their muscles.

▶ They lift every second day in order to give the muscles time to rebuild and recuperate.

▶ They lift to just before the point of exhaustion to prevent overtaxing the muscles.

In sum, they:

▶ Push just past the point of discomfort.

▶ Stop before the point of pain.

▶ Recuperate.

If they continue this process regularly and properly, they will gain the ability to lift more and more weight, and they will gain more and more strength.

The same is true with building resilience to stress:

▶ Seek stressful situations of appropriate intensity (not too intense, but intense enough to stress yourself).

▶ Seek stressful situations of the appropriate duration (not too long, but long enough to feel some stress).

▶ Seek stressful situations at the right frequency (often enough to stress yourself, but not so often that you experience exhaustion).

▶ In between these self-created situations, recover. Do this by relaxing mentally. Always be sure to maintain the "big four" of health: sleep right, eat right, exercise right, and allow time for relaxation.

If you continue to follow this regimen, you will find that you will gradually be able to manage more stress in your life (of greater intensity, or greater duration, and with greater frequency). Eventually, as life continues to throw negative situations, experiences, and other problems your way, you will possess the emotional, mental, and physical strength to cope with them much better than you ever have before.

The easiest way to begin this whole process of building resilience is to manage your day slightly differently. Many people work nonstop for extended periods of time (usually the whole day), then fall exhausted for the rest of the day (usually in the evening).

Try this instead: Work hard for an hour or two. Then take a fifteen-minute break to rest or do something completely different. (If you have a sedentary job, do something physical during your break. If you have a physical job, do something sedentary during your break.) Follow this routine throughout the course of the day. You should find that by evening, you still have lots of energy left, and you may feel motivated to do even more work (of whatever kind you enjoy) in the evening.

As you begin to build this "on-again, off-again" pattern during the day, you will soon get into the routine of stress and recovery, which, again, is the key to building resilience.

In fact, resilience is really the natural order of things. Because life must include both pleasure and pain, to seek pleasure without accepting pain is tantamount to striving for loss of consciousness.

An affirmation that may help: *"That which does not kill me makes me stronger."*

Summary

In this chapter, you learned how to challenge each of the fourteen personality traits that can cause stress, which were outlined in Chapter 3. By identifying the specific traits that trigger the most stress in your life, you learned ways to challenge them and replace them with more constructive ways of viewing situations, with healthier habits, and with new beliefs to prevent the stress response.

CHAPTER SIX

Additional Strategies

This chapter covers a number of additional strategies to cope with stress by:

- ▶ Understanding your personality type
- ▶ Preventing stress before it occurs
- ▶ Dealing with stress while it's occurring
- ▶ Recovering from stress afterward

Personality Type and Stress

Interestingly, your tendency to be either an introvert or an extrovert can determine in what situations you may experience stress. There are tests you can take to determine if you are an introvert or an extrovert. Most people, however, already have a pretty good idea. Since Carl Jung came up with the concepts of introverts and extroverts in *Psychological Types*, published in 1921, this "personality construct" has received a lot of attention.[1]

In simplest terms, extroverts are happiest when they are around other people. In fact, it might be fair to say that they actually need other people. For the most part, extroverts are concerned with the external world of things and people. Well-balanced extroverts tend to be warm, sociable, enthusiastic, adventurous, and active. They actually gain energy from being involved in activities that revolve around being with other people. Many extroverts tend to experience stress when they are alone. They feel bored and cut off from the world, and this can create anxiety.

Introverts, on the other hand, experience happiness from being alone and from having the time to think and create. They have a strong need for inner peace, and being around other people can distract them from this inner peace. For the most part, introverts are concerned with the internal world and with their own ideas and musings. Unlike extroverts, who gain energy from being with other people, introverts lose energy and experience stress when they are around other people. They feel they are "on display" and are expected to "perform" in a certain way. They feel, in many ways, like actors on a stage who have no interest in acting, but who have been forced to stand in front of an audience and "be a part of the play."

Whereas extroverts tend to be swayed and stressed by ever-changing world events (watching the news constantly, talking with other people about stressful world events), well-balanced introverts tend to remain steady and focused on the inner calm and peace within their lives. (Less well-balanced introverts may get caught up in world events and feel helpless in such situations.) Although well-balanced introverts are aware of the turmoil in the world, they are significantly less stressed by it than are extroverts. In fact, while extroverts often find themselves engaging in knee-jerk reactions to the frequent changes that take place in the outer world, introverts can usually sit back and simply observe the changes. They can also sit back and observe the extroverts' reactions to those changes. Rather than react to changes, introverts prefer to analyze them.

Introverts prefer to engage in activities that promote relaxation, such as walking, reading, sitting on a back porch, watching trees sway in the breeze, and listening to music. They experience stress when they are in loud, crowded places.

Extroverts, on the other hand, thrive in the loud, crowded places. After all, they are "home." They are around other people. For the most part, extroverts need constant encouragement and attention, which they attempt to generate from public reaction. They experience stress when they are ignored.

Introverts, are quite capable of providing their own encouragement. This comes from deep within, and it allows them to concentrate on "their work" without need for external approval or encouragement. In fact, they often experience stress if they are forced into the limelight. A classic example is Boo Radley (an introvert) in *To Kill a Mockingbird*. Imagine Mr. T (an extrovert) playing that role! After saving Jim from attack at the end of the movie, Mr. T would have the media on the phone, telling his story to the world. Boo Radley, on the other hand, cowered behind a door in a dark room.

One of the most stressful experiences for an introvert is not being understood by extroverts. That is, although introverts tend to find it relatively easy to understand extroverts and what makes them tick (given the fact that they spend the majority of their lives observing them in action), it is extremely difficult for extroverts to understand introverts. After all, extroverts are too busy being with people (primarily other extroverts) to try to understand people who rarely make their presence known. "Why don't they like to spend time with people like I do?" the extrovert will ask. "Why aren't they normal like me?"

As such, conversely, extroverts may get stressed being around introverts, who often seem antisocial and come across as downers in a "fun" situation (fun for the extroverts, that is).

Generally, introverts prefer to feel relaxed. They tend to seek foods, activities, and situations that increase brain levels of serotonin (a neurotransmitter that promotes relaxation), which provides a sense of safety, relaxation, and satiation.

Conversely, extroverts prefer to be excited, aroused, and in a heightened state of alertness. They tend to adopt behaviors that increase brain levels of dopamine (a neurotransmitter that promotes excitation), in order to experience a more consistent state of arousal.

Any prolonged experience of the nonpreferred condition will trigger stress. Thus, for introverts, any prolonged state of arousal can be stressful. Conversely, for extroverts, any prolonged state of calm or boredom can generate stress.

Although well-balanced introverts prefer solitude, they are able to balance this with social interactions. Some introverts, however, can become too reclusive. This retreat threatens to weaken their self-confidence and leads them to believe that they are too weak to handle social interaction. They lead themselves to believe that they lack the vitality and courage necessary to interact with others. This fear can generate even more stress for such introverts than actually being in public and interacting with other people.

It's no secret that extroverts rule the world in at least two ways. First, in terms of sheer numbers, extroverts outnumber introverts by about three to one. Second, since extroverts are so much more vocal, visible, sociable, and easier to understand (given their penchant for communicating), they tend to dominate events; activities; and, for that matter, society in general. In sum, the extrovert's goal is to be with people and to be social, and society is geared toward helping them do this, because the majority of society thinks the same way.

Introverts, on the other hand, with their quiet ways and their private lives, are forced as the minority to seek refuge from extroverted society and find time for themselves.

In addition, it is difficult for extroverts to understand introverts. In fact, given the cultural leaning toward extraversion and the mistaken belief among so many introverts that they should become extroverts, many introverts often find it difficult to understand each other. That is, while extroverts like to spend time with other extroverts, introverts like to spend time with themselves. They don't even want to spend much time with other introverts. In sum, few people really understand introverts, except introverts themselves.

Different conversation styles can also generate stress for introverts and extroverts. Introverts often prefer long conversations about one topic, where they have the opportunity to really get into what they are saying and, conversely, really get into listening to what the other person is saying. They frequently experience stress when conversing with extroverts, who like to interrupt and/or change the topic of conversation frequently. Introverts perceive the interruption and shift in topic as a sign that the extroverts are not interested in them. In sum, they take it personally.

Extroverts, on the other hand, prefer short, snappy, back-and-forth conversations with frequent topic shifts. They experience stress when they feel they are being forced to listen to an introvert go on and on and on about one topic.

Introverts need to realize that when extroverts want to talk about something else, it is not that they aren't interested in the introverts as people. They are interested in them as people. It is simply that they want to explore other topics with them. They find it difficult to stay focused on one topic because their brains are wired to need more stimulation, which comes from multiple topics.

Being an introvert, it took me years to recognize this. I assumed that because I enjoyed listening to people talk at length and really get in depth about something, they would also enjoy hearing the same from me. I took it personally when people seemed less than interested in having me discuss a topic for more than a couple of minutes. Understanding the difference between extroverts and introverts helped me eliminate a long-held resentment I had toward people in general.

However, it didn't eliminate the fact that I still needed a way to explore my thoughts, ideas, and concepts in detail. As such, I realized that the best way for me to make sense of my inner self was not to expect other people to listen to me, but rather to have a conversation with myself each night as I was out running or walking. I am now able to get myself into a light trance, select a topic I want to address, and converse with myself in a state of light meditation for half an hour to an hour. I virtually always come up with exactly the insights I need. I then write these insights in my journal when I return home so I don't forget them.

Now that I understand how other people operate and now that I have also figured out a way to get my own needs met, I am able to communicate with other people in a much more relaxed and less stressful way. Now, when I talk with people, I purposely keep the topics superficial and simple. If they interrupt me, I don't care. The message they are sending me is, "I'm not interested in the topic you're taking about. I want to talk about something else." This is radically different from the message I assumed they were sending before when they interrupted me, which was: "I'm not interested in you."

This still doesn't prevent me from listening to other people when they want to talk about themselves, though. I have always enjoyed it when people opened up, and I still do. When I meet another introvert who wants to "think out loud" with a lengthy discussion about an issue he or she is exploring, I thoroughly enjoy participating in the person's "verbal journey."

Due to societal conditioning, it should come as no surprise that a lot of introverts feel as though they should try to fit into the extrovert's world. They have been led to believe that an extroverted life is expected, "normal," and "the thing to do." More significantly, they often feel as though something is missing from their lives if they remain introverts. They think they should feel the need for other people to fill "something" inside of them, when, in fact, deep down inside, they really don't need that external something. All they need is already within them. This "searching for something they can't define" can generate massive amounts of chronic stress for the introvert.

Introverts may need other people to some extent, but nowhere near as much as they have been socialized to believe they do. Introverts need to learn that it is OK to be who they are. They need to feel free to give up any need they might feel to continue to try to fit into the extrovert's world. They need to learn that it is OK to live and thrive in healthy solitude. It's a different way of living, but it can be truly fulfilling, for the simple reason that it is the natural way of living for them.

When extroverts feel empty, they know they can "fill themselves up" by being around other people. Unfortunately, introverts have been led to believe the same thing—that they need other people to fill them up when they are depleted. When this strategy doesn't work for them (and it doesn't, if they are truly introverts), they feel even more empty and begin to believe that there is something wrong with them. "Most other people cure their emptiness by being around other people. Why can't I?" they ask.

The solution for the introvert is to accept the fact that extroverts can, indeed, get filled up from other people. However, they also need to accept the fact that this is not the way for them to fill up themselves. The way for the introvert to fill up is to "go inside"—to find fulfillment from within, not from other people.

As noted earlier, there is very little guidance for introverts on how to be happy in life. Society seems to suggest that all people, regardless of personality type, can only be happy when they are socializing. More significantly, there is also very little guidance for introverts on the value of going inside; how rewarding it can be; and, most important, how to do so.

Other Ways to Deal with Stress Beforehand

Although the two most important and effective steps in preventing stress are improving your health (Chapter 4) and reframing your perceptions (Chapter 5), there are some other things you can do in this area.

Find Your Excitement Level

Much of what was discussed in Chapters 3 and 5 focused indirectly on the concept of "excitement level." It is important to clarify this concept. Each person has a level of life excitement that is natural for him or her. That is, some people have a high level, meaning they prefer fast-paced, urban, high-pressure lives. If they experience anything less, they can become stressed from boredom. Others have a low level, preferring relaxed, often rural, low-pressure lives. If they are forced to live in a high-pressure environment, they will become stressed.

Find what is natural for you. Then work to get your day-to-day life to match your natural style. Remember, there is no right or wrong. Some people in fast-paced lives think that people living relaxed lives are missing the boat. Conversely, some people living relaxed lives think people living fast-paced lives are insane.

The only thing that is insane is if you are living a life other than the one that is natural for you.

Experience Happiness

This may seem like a no-brainer, but being happy can have a significant impact on the amount of stress you experience. More specifically, find things in your life that make you happy. When you live the majority of your life feeling good, chemicals course through your body that help prevent stress responses. In addition, when you're happy, you tend to eat better, exercise more, and sleep better. Overall, a positive frame of mind is an excellent way to reduce stressful reactions.

Build Social Ties

People who have a lot of friends, or at least a strong social network and people with whom to interact (including family), tend to experience less stress than people who feel alone or abandoned in life. Communication helps you sort out experiences in your life that otherwise could go unresolved. As unresolved issues build up, pressure builds up, and as pressure builds up, you make yourself more susceptible to stress.

Simplify Your Life

For many people, this is easier said than done. Some people just don't feel human if they're not involved in a million things. For them, even if they make a conscious effort to stop and smell the roses, it can take years for their hearts to catch up to their heads (to feel comfortable relaxing, even though their brains have been telling them to do it for years).

Here are some specific ways to do less:

▶ Ask yourself what really needs to be done. In other words, ask yourself: If I don't perform this specific task right now, what will the consequences be? Management guru Peter Drucker, for example, has said that 80 percent of what is done in the workplace is the result of habit, not need.

▶ Cut down on the number of people to whom you give your e-mail address, unless you really love e-mail. I have talked with business executives who say they spend one-third of their days reading and responding to e-mails, most of which are irrelevant.

I learned about the latter firsthand when, after two years of resisting the technology because of the horror stories I had heard about wasted time, I began using e-mail. I thought about inform-ing all of the more than forty editors I worked with that I had it, but felt it was wiser to try an experiment first. I gave my e-mail address to just one editor, a man for whom I have been writing for twenty-five years. During that time, I sent him between one and five articles a month, every month. Not once in those twenty-five years did he ever take the time to type and mail a letter to me telling me he had received my articles. Not once did he take the time to pick up the phone to call and tell me he had received my articles. Not once did he take the time to type a fax and send it to me, telling me he had received my articles. It wasn't necessary, because I always knew he'd received the articles when I got paid. Yet, a week after I got e-mail, I received an e-mail message from him, telling me he had received my articles and thanking me for sending them. I thought to myself: "That's a waste of time—his time in writing it and sending it, my time in having to download it and read it." I didn't think anything more about it until we were talking on the phone a couple of weeks later about some new article ideas. He said, "Did you get my e-mail?" "The one about receiving my articles?" I responded. "Yeah," he said. "Yeah, I got it," I added. There was a pause on the line. Then he said, "Well, you're supposed to respond to those things!"

Redefine TV Habits

Stop watching the news (or what the media calls "news"). My definition of news is information that, once you see or hear it, causes you to do something different with your life than you were previously doing, or causes you to continue to do something that you might have otherwise given up. New medical research on how to stay healthy, for example, is something I consider news. Virtually everything else is just a perverse form of entertainment designed to twist your emotions into a knot.

Certainly, there are exceptions. It's news when the news stations (CNN and Fox News) skip commercials in order to stay with a story, or when the three major networks (ABC, CBS, and NBC) break into regularly scheduled programming to report a story. As such, the terrorist attacks and subsequent anthrax illnesses were important news, because they either directly or indirectly affected our lives and the decisions we needed to make in our lives.

Again, though, most of what is reported as news is designed to keep you stressed out. If something is important enough to know about, you'll hear about it somehow. You don't need to let the media twist your emotions into a knot every night for no reason.

Along the same lines, select your other TV programming carefully. Ask yourself before you watch a show: Is this show positive, upbeat, and life affirming? Or is it negative, downbeat, and pandering to the sordid? If, at the end of a show, you feel better about life and the human race in general, then it was a good choice. Expect your stress levels to decrease over the next twenty-four hours. On the other hand, if you feel worse about life and the human race, then you have done yourself a disservice. Expect your stress levels to increase over the next twenty-four hours.

Notice Color

This may seem like an odd recommendation, but there is some credible research to suggest that the colors with which you surround yourself directly affect your mood. For example, there are three colors that are particularly conducive to relaxation and stress reduction, plus three colors that have the opposite effect. They are listed here from most calming to least calming, with their characteristics in parentheses: blue (calming, elevates mood, creates happiness), brown (calming, reduces blood pressure), pink (lowers blood pressure, reduces aggression and hostility), green (increases stress), yellow (stimulating, increases alertness), and red (stimulating, increases stress and arousal).

Ways to Deal with Stress During Stress

When you are faced with a potentially stressful situation, here are some strategies to implement to cope more effectively.

Reflect

Ask yourself: "What would a calm person do in this situation?" Then, do it! If a calm person would do nothing, then do nothing.

Smile

In most cases, if you're being genuine, your face reflects your mood. That is, if you're happy, your face looks happy. If you're stressed, your face looks stressed. However, your face can do more than reflect your mood. It can *affect* your mood. That is, if you fake it by putting on the face you want, your physiology will respond by working to create that mood for real. As such, if you're stressed, relax and create the facial features of someone who is relaxed. You will then gradually begin to feel more relaxed.

Slow Down

Purposely move in slow motion (or "slower motion"). If you're in a stressful situation and feel compelled to move quickly (a la "running around like a chicken with its head cut off"), slow down to a more normal speed. Again, faking it like this can lead to reality. Your physiology and your mind will respond by becoming calmer. If you're alone, you may actually want to experiment with moving in slow motion. (You obviously don't want to do this in public, or people will think you've lost it.)

Laugh

Just as humor can be helpful in *preventing* stress (discussed in Chapter 5), it can be equally helpful during stressful situations (discussed here), and even in decompressing from stressful situations (discussed in the "Ways to Deal with Stress Afterward" section). Laughter releases catecholamines into the bloodstream, which improve your alertness and mental functioning, thus allowing you to react better to situations. Furthermore, laughter helps reduce blood pressure. It also oxygenates the blood and relaxes your muscles. Finally, it creates T cells, which strengthen your immune system.

Some recommendations from humor professional Joel Goodman:

- People say, "Some day we'll laugh about this." Goodman asks, "Why wait?"

- Ask yourself how your favorite comedian would handle this situation. How would Jerry Seinfeld cover it in a show? How would Erma Bombeck have written about it?

Ways to Deal with Stress Afterward

Theoretically, if you follow all of the recommendations up to this point, you should never experience another stressful moment in your life. That, however, is obviously unrealistic, so here are some recommendations for decompressing when you do need to recover from stress. They are divided into four categories.

Passive Things You Can Do Yourself

Here are five recommendations:

1. Watch television or a video (preferably a comedy or other light form of entertainment that puts you in an up-beat mood).

2. Read a book (again, something humorous or entertaining that makes you laugh or at least smile).

3. Listen to music. Music affects the most primitive part of the brain, which regulates heart rate, respiration, and muscle tension. As such, listen to something soothing.

4. Relax and do nothing. Sit and do nothing. Sit in the park and watch children play. Sit on your back porch and watch the birds.

5. Sit in total quiet and hear that still, small voice inside that helps you create perspective.

Active Things You Can Do Yourself

If you enjoy gardening, do so. If you enjoy woodworking, do so. If you enjoy decorating your house, do so. Consider a walk in nature. (This has a very calming effect.) If you enjoy none of these, then you may be forced into a last resort—exercise! You may hate it, but it's the best thing for you (other than a good night's sleep).

Consider journaling. This is especially useful for wrestling with issues that you may feel uncomfortable discussing with friends, family, or even a counselor, but that you need to address one way or another. Write for about twenty minutes a day, free-flowing and uncensored. Don't worry about grammar, spelling, paragraph structure, or other rules English teachers taught you. Free-form writing allows you to get on a roll.

The first benefit of journaling is that it acts as an emotional release. Second, it can ultimately lead to some new insights about why you are stressed and how you can put things into perspective and handle things differently next time. One study showed that people who wrote about stressful experiences reported fewer stress symptoms, had fewer days off from work and fewer visits to the doctor, and ended up with more positive outlooks in general.

Passive Things You Can Do with Others

Probably the most useful recommendation here is to arrange for a massage. If you can't talk your spouse or children into giving you one, hire a professional. Massages improve circulation, reduce the buildup of waste material in the muscles and bloodstream (primarily lactic acid), and ultimately relax your muscles.

Active Things You Can Do with Others

The best recommendation here is to *talk*. Talk with a friend or family member. If no one will listen to you, hire a counselor. Besides helping you gain perspective and insights, the opportunity to talk about what has been stressing you out also has been shown to reduce blood pressure.

Summary

In this chapter, you learned some additional strategies to help address stress in your life. One related to understanding how introverts and extroverts respond differently to stress. Another related to additional stress-prevention steps. You also learned about some steps to take to reduce the stress experience while it is occurring, as well as some steps to take to decompress from stress after it has occurred. Ideally, of course, if you are successful with all of the other strategies, then there will be less and less need to decompress from stress over time, since it will be occurring less and less in your life.

PART III

Advanced Stress-Prevention Strategies

Part II reviewed a number of basic steps you can take to begin to prevent stress in your life. Part III will focus on three advanced steps you can take.

I recommend that you spend sufficient time mastering the steps in Part II before taking on the additional tasks of mastering the steps in Part III. (See Part IV—"The 100-Day Plan.")

The first step in Part III is to begin a chi kung program. This is a program based on the Far Eastern principles of "chi"—energy. Although occasional chi kung practice can be effective in reducing stress, daily chi kung practice can be effective in building your resilience in such a way that it actually helps to prevent the stress response.

The second step is to start a meditation program. Although some people equate meditation with certain religions, it can be a completely nonreligious exercise. And as with chi kung, occasional meditation can be effective in reducing stress, while daily meditation can help prevent the stress response.

The third step is, admittedly, a sensitive and complex one. It involves completely rethinking what is real in your life. It focuses on adopting spiritual beliefs and practices that help you realize that what you consider the real world (the physical world) is actually an illusion, and the spiritual world (that "something else out there") is the true reality. By being able to shift more and more of your consciousness to the spiritual world, you will experience less and less stress from the real world, because you will realize that nothing that happens in the real world matters. In fact, I would propose that this step, although possibly the most challenging, is actually the most effective step in preventing stress in your life.

CHAPTER SEVEN

Generating Positive Energy from Chi

One of the most effective ways to prevent stress in your life is to build up your internal energy system to such a degree that it is difficult for the physiological stress response to even occur. Although engaging in traditional Western exercises such as running or weight lifting can build internal energy to some extent, we really have to explore an Eastern tradition to find a way to build boundless internal energy.

Understanding Chi

The concept is called "chi," and the exercise is "chi kung" (often spelled "chi gong" or "qigong").

The Chinese believe that there are "energy meridians," which run through our bodies, as well as "energy vessels," which store and direct the energy that flows through the meridians. They call this energy chi, or the "vital life force."

Westerners often find the concept difficult to understand.

After all, no one can see chi, so why would one believe that it exists? Probably the easiest way to introduce the concept is to think about three people, one who is vibrant and healthy, one who is near death, and one who has recently died. The first person is said to have a good supply of chi. The person near death has very little chi left. The person who has just died has no chi at all. In fact, think about the transition from life to death. What has actually changed when a person's body dies? One minute, the person is alive. The next, the person is dead. The most dramatic difference, according to the Chinese, is that the chi has left the body of the dead person.

If the concept is still difficult to grasp, think about houseplants. When they are alive with energy, there is a natural tension that keeps the leaves and stems strong enough to defy gravity and point upward or outward. However, if the plant begins to die, the chi gradually leaves the plant. You become aware of this because the stems lose their strength and begin to bend, and the leaves lose their rigidity and begin to droop. This can happen even before the leaves start turning brown. The bending and drooping are signs that the plant's chi is getting weak.

The Chinese believe that by engaging in certain chi-building practices, you can gradually strengthen the mind and body to attain health and longevity and, at the same time, generate so much internal energy that your mind and body end up becoming virtually immune to the physiological stress response and the mental processes that generate it.

The Chinese believe that there are three levels of energy in the body. These are "jing" (generative energy), "chi" (vital energy), and "shen" (spirit energy). For purposes of convenience in the discussion here, all three energies when discussed as one are referred to as chi.

When a healthy, normal child is born, all three energies are strong. As the infant grows into adulthood and eventually old age, though, the three energies gradually begin to dissipate. Jing is lost via excessive sexual activity, chi is lost via excessive emotions, and shen is lost via excessive mental activity. As these energies decline, the body's overall level of energy declines, leading to, for some people, chronic illness. Eventually, though, for everyone, death occurs.

In sum, a normal, healthy baby has more energy (not physical strength, of course) than anyone at any other age. I recall hearing a story in my youth about Jim Thorpe, the world-class Olympic athlete from the 1910s and 1920s who was considered the most physically fit person in the world at the time. It is said that he was asked to mimic the activities of an infant for as long as he could. He supposedly collapsed from exhaustion after less than an hour, but the infant was still going strong! Hard to believe? Try it yourself. You'll be lucky to last ten minutes. Healthy infants are brimming with chi!

We all know people in their thirties who seem so low on energy that they seem as though they're in their seventies. They are chronically ill, often because they burn the candle at both ends, abuse their bodies and their minds, and spend no time regenerating themselves with healthy habits. These are people who end up suffering from low libido (low jing levels), chronic fatigue (low chi levels), and mental lethargy or confusion (low shen levels).

Conversely, we know people in their eighties who seem to have boundless energy and a love for life. These are people who have learned to carefully manage the use of their energy and also intuitively found ways to replace it. Obviously, these people (at least those in the Western world) have not learned to replace their energy via chi kung practices.

You, too, may be able to live a long and energetic life without adopting chi kung practices. However, the benefit of chi kung is that you can accomplish the same results, but compress the energy-rebuilding process into a short period of time. While it may take most people three or four hours to rebuild their energy by taking relaxing walks, fishing, enjoying time with friends, or whatever they do to rekindle their energy, you can rebuild the same amount of energy with fifteen minutes of chi kung practice a day. And by practicing thirty minutes a day, you can create even more energy than you expend, leading to a situation where you get healthier with each passing year, rather than less healthy!

In sum, what chi kung does is to restore the three energies that are lost due to depletions that occur during the stresses and strains of everyday living.

According to Chinese tradition:

Jing is stored in the adrenal cortex and the sexual organs. There are three basic elements of jing. One is blood and the vital elements carried in the bloodstream, including nutrients. The second is hormones, which are secreted by various glands and regulate growth, metabolism, sexuality, immunity, and aging. These include male and female hormones, as well as sperm and ova. The third is essential (heavy) fluids, such as lymph and joint lubricants, tears, perspiration, and urine. Jing is depleted via stress, sexual activity, malnutrition, and illness. The ways to replenish jing are maintain a healthy diet, drink large quantities of water, and engage in chi kung exercise. (Most people simply do not get enough water. In fact, one of the most common causes of body deterioration over the years is lack of sufficient hydration. You should drink enough water so that you are producing clear urine every one to two hours. Of course, you want to taper off drinking in the evening so you won't be up all night!)

Chi is stored in the heart and is manifested as breath, heat, and pulse. Chi is depleted most commonly by excess emotions, especially pensiveness, surprise, anger, grief/sorrow, fear, worry, and stress. It can also be depleted by improper breathing techniques (short and shallow breathing) and/or breathing polluted air. Chi can be restored by healthy food, water, supplements, proper breathing (discussed later), and chi kung practice.

Shen resides in the pineal gland (which is located in the brain but is not actually a part of the brain). Shen includes all mental faculties, including thought, intuition, spirit, will, and ego. Shen can become scattered and weak when bombarded by mental disturbances, such as a large ego, attachment to objects (possessiveness), frequent mental agitation, and narrow-mindedness (having a closed mind, discriminating, etc.). It can be rejuvenated via meditation (discussed in Chapter 8) and by chi kung practice.

Chi Kung

Chi kung practice is designed first to strengthen jing, which is gradually refined and then stored in the abdomen, the center of the body's energy. As you build more jing, the excess then goes to begin to build chi, which is also refined and then stored. The excess chi is then used to build shen, which leads to a feeling of almost perfect peace (a life with no stress).

Chi kung is actually "exerciseless exercise." In its most basic form, it involves standing—just standing. Although the details of what to do and how to do it are covered later, it is important to first understand the different approaches to exercise. The Western world focuses almost exclusively on active exercise. Eastern culture focuses on active and passive exercise, seeing benefits to the passive forms of exercise that the Western world just doesn't seem to understand.

Active exercise (running, weight lifting, etc.) develops bones, muscles, and other elements that show in the outer physique. It is designed to build strength and endurance. The feeling of strength and power, though, results from alternate muscular contraction and relaxation. The Chinese, however, believe that this muscular contraction prevents the free flow of chi. For example, a person may be able to do 100 push-ups, run a marathon, and exhibit a fit shape but internally suffer from a number of illnesses and injuries, including heart disease, cancer, and diabetes. In other words, although the outside seems to be healthy, the inside can be unhealthy. Take the example of bodybuilders. Although many people believe that the veins popping out from under the skin is a sign of health, it is actually a sign of damage. The muscles have become so hard that the veins are unable to carry blood and other nutrients through the body anymore. They are thus forced to pop to the surface, gasping for air and the opportunity to continue flowing.

Chi kung (motionless exercise), on the other hand, develops "effortless power," looseness, and flexibility. A person who practices chi kung may look frail and unmuscular, even overweight, however actually be the picture of health inside.

Traditional anaerobic exercise (e.g., weight lifting) stretches muscles, but they always shrink back. Chi kung allows muscles to stretch naturally, then remain in a relaxed state. In chi kung, power results from muscles being able to loosen, open up, and allow energy to flow through them.

Traditional aerobic exercise (e.g., running) increases circulation by exercising the heart. Chi kung improves circulation by increasing the elasticity of the muscles and blood vessels so that the heart does not need to work as hard in the first place.

Traditional exercise creates blockages by hardening muscles, which leads to feelings of strength, but which actually prevents the normal, healthy, steady flow of energy through the body. In other words, the stronger you feel muscularly, the weaker your chi is! Chi kung, on the other hand, helps create a relaxed, comfortable, balanced feeling and allows energy to flow freely through all parts of the body.

Traditional exercise creates tension, which activates the nerves, which signals the muscles to contract, which shortens the muscles (pulling on the insertion points where they attach to the bones and ligaments), which causes strain and fatigue, which causes blood circulation to diminish in this area, which blocks the chi in your energy channels, which causes pain, which causes more tension, and so on and so on.

Chi kung, on the other hand, allows muscles to stretch and nerves to release, which lessens tension. Relaxation allows the muscles and nerves to maintain a smooth flow of energy. Chi kung helps to lengthen habitually contracted, tight, shortened muscles and tendons. The relaxation comes from mentally letting go of the habitual tension in the nerves.

The body needs nerve strength to be able to tell the muscles to continually and gently lengthen in the appropriate ways. In other words, nerve strength, not muscular strength, is required in order to remain upright. Nerve relaxation leads to muscle relaxation. Once you achieve deep relaxation, the weight of the soft tissue and bodily fluids will gradually and gently pull on your other soft tissues, including ligaments, tendons, and muscle fascia. This gentle pulling without tension gradually stretches soft tissues and thus lengthens them.

Abdominal Breathing

Before beginning chi kung practice, it is important to learn to breathe properly, not only during chi kung practice, but throughout the day.

If you look at a baby lying on the floor, you will notice that it has a huge, distended belly. This isn't fat. This is the result of natural (abdominal) breathing. Babies breathe very deeply, which is the natural way to breathe and which nourishes the body with all of the oxygen that it needs.

As we grow, though, stress, anxiety, worry, fear, anger, and other negative emotions cause us to gradually begin subconsciously breathing more quickly. In order to breathe quickly, though, we first must shift from deep breathing (the natural breathing we use as infants) to shallow breathing. In order to engage in shallow breathing, we must stop breathing from the abdomen (as we did as infants), and begin breathing at the chest level, just below the throat. In other words, we cannot breathe quickly when we breathe abdominally. As such, most of us, over the years, begin to develop the habit of breathing at the chest level (the upper and narrow area of the lungs), so that we can engage in quick, shallow breathing.

The problem is that this type of breathing prevents physical, emotional, and mental relaxation. In other words, the breathing itself triggers physical, emotional, and mental tension. This becomes a vicious cycle, because the physical, emotional, and mental tension encourage continued short and shallow breathing. Just as importantly, shallow breathing compromises your health, because it fails to provide sufficient oxygen for the blood to circulate throughout the body and properly nourish all of the muscles, glands, organs, bones, and other parts of the body.

The way to break this negative cycle is to begin to set aside two or three minutes several times a day to stop and "catch yourself breathing." As you notice your quick and shallow chest breathing, slow down. Begin to breathe slowly and deeply, purposely expanding your lower abdomen (in the area of your stomach). Until this form of breathing becomes natural again (I say "again," because this is the way you used to breathe when you were an infant), you will have to actually force your abdominal muscles to expand and contract. Inhale deeply until your abdomen is fully extended and your lower lungs are completely filled. Then exhale slowly, pulling your abdomen back in, and pushing out all of the air from your lower lungs.

Do this for two or three minutes at a time, four or five times a day. Then gradually increase your time and your frequency, until you are up to five minutes at a time once every hour or so during the day. If you practice this diligently, a miracle will happen. You will eventually begin to breathe this way again naturally, and you won't even be aware of it, until you happen to catch yourself breathing and say to yourself, "My goodness! I am breathing deeply and slowly in my abdomen!"

As you experience the transformation in breathing, you will find that your levels of stress and anxiety begin to diminish concurrently. Again, as noted earlier, quick and shallow breathing generates tension, which generates more quick and shallow breathing. Slow, deep, abdominal breathing, on the other hand, generates relaxation and reduces the stress response, which, subsequently, continues to encourage more slow, deep, abdominal breathing.

I was a quick, shallow breather for virtually all of my adult life. About ten years ago, I began to consciously practice abdominal breathing, expecting that I would have to practice it for the rest of my life. However, within about three months, I found that it had become a habit, and I now breathe this way all of the time. In fact, I would have to make a significant effort to try to engage in short, shallow, chest breathing again.

One result of abdominal breathing that some people may not like is that you end up with what looks like a "gut." That is, if you're committed to learning to breathe properly, forget about being able to sport "six-pack abs." It won't happen. However, if you recall the earlier discussion of the differences between Western (active) exercise and Eastern (passive) exercise, you won't want "six-pack abs" anyway. They are manifestations of tight, tense, hard muscles, which prevent the free flow of energy.

Your "gut," on the other hand, is a manifestation of your relaxed abdomen that is free to breathe expansively in and out. Easterners refer to it as the "Buddha belly." (If you have ever seen certain pictures or statues of Buddha, you will recall that he has a big smile on his face and a huge gut! It's not from overeating. It's from abdominal breathing.)

If you aren't sure whether your distended abdomen is the result of relaxed breathing or excessive eating, there is a test you can perform. Lie on the ground, and suck your belly in as tightly as you can. If you still see massive mounds of flesh, then you have a fat problem (quite possibly caused by stress, as noted in Chapter 1). On the other hand, if everything disappears and you can see your stomach depress lower than your rib cage, then congratulations. You have a relaxed abdomen.

Now, the only problem is explaining that to family, friends, and neighbors, who may be thinking to themselves, "Bob really needs to lose some weight!" However, if you end up reaching the enlightened state (which you can do by lengthy practice of chi kung, meditation, and some other spiritual practices covered here and in Chapters 8 and 9), your ego will disintegrate, and you really won't care what anyone else thinks of your belly.

Once you have begun practicing abdominal breathing, you're ready to begin actual chi kung practice.

Chi Kung Practice

There are several very lengthy and detailed instructions to begin chi kung practice. It will take time to understand all of them, remember all of them, and feel comfortable with all of them. In fact, as you are learning them, it may take you five or ten minutes just to prepare yourself for a chi kung session. However, over time, and as you practice more, these preparation habits will become second nature, and you will get to the point where you will actually be able to prepare for a chi kung session within seconds. It's no different than driving a car. When you first learn, you are overwhelmed with all of the things you have to do. You sit in the driveway stupefied by all of the steps you have to go through to start the car and begin moving, and it takes quite a while to get moving. That's the way it should be, as you are training your mind in new habits. After a while, though, starting the car becomes second nature, and you can do it in a few seconds without even thinking about the steps you take.

Step 1

As is true with so many other relaxation techniques, it is important to create the proper environment for chi kung practice. The usual rules apply: loose clothing, a quiet room where you won't be disturbed, and darkness or semidarkness.

You may also consider some relaxing and quiet music. Some people find this facilitates their concentration. Others find that it distracts from it. Experiment.

Step 2

Relax. There are two levels of relaxation. The first is to relax yourself externally (your posture, your facial features, etc.). The second is to relax yourself internally (your muscles and tendons). (The Chinese also have a third level, which involves relaxing the internal organs. However, this takes years of practice and is beyond the scope and purpose of this book.)

There are three steps to achieving deep relaxation. You must relax your mind, relax your breathing, and relax your body.

When you relax your mind, you can relax your lungs. When you relax your lungs, you can breathe properly. When you can breathe properly, you can slow your heartbeat. When you slow your heartbeat, you can relax your mind more. When you relax your mind more, you can relax your lungs more. And so on, and so on.

To relax your mind, bring all of your thoughts from the outside world to your body. Allow all of your thoughts to be calm and peaceful. Disregard surrounding distractions. Although your mind may be clear, it may be tense from concentration. Learn to concentrate without mental tension. Do this by focusing on your deep, abdominal breathing—the sensation of your lungs expanding and contracting. As you exhale, feel your body relax to a deeper level.

To relax your breathing, relax your abdomen so that it can expand and contract freely. (Refer back to the "Abdominal Breathing" section.)

To relax your body, sense the muscles in your body, especially those that are tight. Allow your breathing and calm mind to help relax the tension in the muscles.

Step 3

Relax your facial muscles. Then smile gently.

Step 4

Stand in position properly. First, spread your legs out in what is called a "horse stance," which means that your feet are positioned directly below imaginary vertical lines dropping down from the outside of your shoulders. For most people, this will mean that your feet are about sixteen to twenty inches apart (measured from the inside of one foot to the inside of the other foot). Second, plant your feet so that they are facing straight forward, not pointed inward or outward. This may feel uncomfortable at first, but the stabilization it provides will eventually begin to feel very comfortable and natural. This posture is also necessary to sustain the energy levels used in chi kung practice.

Step 5

Flex your knees. This is *very* important. Do not stand with your legs in a rigid position! It prevents the chi from being able to flow completely through the body. In addition, it will build artificial tension that will exhaust you within a short period of time, preventing you from engaging in extended chi kung sessions. Flex your knees slightly, but not so much that your knees extend out farther forward than your toes. Again, this flexing is necessary to allow the muscles and blood vessels to remain relaxed in the legs, which will facilitate the eventual flow of chi down and back up the legs.

After you gain more experience practicing chi, you can gradually bend your knees even farther, squatting lower and lower (but still with your knees not extending past your toes). This involves keeping your back straight and lowering your rump. The lower you go, the more forcefully you will be able to move your chi. It is an experience difficult to describe, but you will know it once you begin to experience it.

However, again, don't try the deep posture at first. It will only cause you to tense up, lose your balance, and prevent your chi from flowing.

You will know you are at the right height when you can pretend you are pushing a heavy object upward. That is, select the height where you feel you can push upward most strongly. This is also the point where you can exert the strongest push downward. When you have found this midway point, you are flexing properly.

Again, though, over time, as you gain more endurance and energy, you will be able to sink lower and experience the same feeling of upward and downward pushing strength.

Step 6

Distribute weight on your feet properly. As much as possible, distribute your weight evenly across the bottom of your feet. Do not place your weight either to the outside or the inside, or on the balls or heels of your feet. Maximizing ground contact in this way helps to facilitate balance.

Visualize a line dropping from the top of your head, down through the core of your body, behind your knees (since your knees are flexed forward), and ending at the bottom of your feet in the center. This should provide stable balance and ultimate relaxation.

In the early stages of chi kung practice, you must achieve this posture of being physically balanced, centered, and stable. It will help you become mentally centered during chi practice.

After you have gained some experience, though, you can practice being physically unbalanced, uncentered, and unstable while maintaining your mental balance, centeredness, and stability.

Step 7

Allow your arms to hang loosely by your sides. Bend your elbows out very slightly, so that your forearms will angle slightly inward toward the outsides of your thighs.

Relax your fingers, and allow them to remain separated from each other, flexed just slightly like your knees and elbows (rather than straight and rigid).

Step 8

Look straight ahead. Stare either at a blank wall or at a large, calming picture, so as not to be distracted. Another option is to close your eyes. As noted in Step 1, it is useful to have the lights either very low or off to prevent distraction. So what's the point of having a calming picture in front of you if you can't even see it? It's psychological. If you know there is something calming in front of you, even if you can't see it for the moment, it promotes a sense of calm.

Experiment with light levels, pictures, and eyes open or closed until you find the combination that helps you generate the strongest flow of chi.

Step 9

As you begin to stand, become aware of places in your body where you feel pain, tension, constriction, weakness, and other discomfort. These are all of the places where chi is unable to flow—where it is blocked. In fact, these are places where disease and illness can begin. By gently loosening these tight areas, chi, blood, and nutrients will flow more freely and smoothly through these areas, once again nourishing them and reducing the potential for illness.

To begin to identify these areas, focus carefully on your body. Get inside of yourself, and become aware of all parts of your body. This leads to an incredibly high level of physical sensitivity. I like to call it "body scanning." When you engage in this kind of concentrated, sensitive focus, you can feel things that you would not otherwise feel. For example, if you have an ingrown toenail that you never noticed, body scanning should begin to make the area throb in great pain. If you have recently cut yourself and the wound is healing, you may not be aware of the pain most of the time. However, once you begin to body scan, this area should throb with pain.

This is all a good sign. It means that your mind is becoming intensely sensitive to your body. When this happens, you will be able to identify areas of your body that are not completely healthy. These will be areas where you will eventually be able to direct chi to facilitate the healing process.

When I first started body scanning a few years ago, I began to feel a stabbing pain in the bottom of my foot. It hurt intensely when I was scanning, but I never even noticed the pain at all any other time. I felt the area and noticed a small, hard lump, as though something were underneath the skin. I pulled at the skin with a pair of tweezers and eventually felt something very hard. It was a sliver-thin piece of glass about a quarter inch long! I must have stepped on it years earlier and forgotten about it. When I removed the glass, the wound healed quickly, and within a couple of weeks, there was no pain at all in that area during scanning.

Another time as I was body scanning, I began to feel a stabbing pain on the right side of my chest. Over the course of the next three or four weeks as I was focusing chi in that area, a small lump about the size of a pinhead developed just under the skin. A couple of days later, the skin broke open, and a small steel pellet (slightly larger than a pinhead) emerged! I have no idea how it ended up in my body, but body scanning and chi practice helped to identify it, sensitize the muscles in that area to its presence, and help them to gradually work it outward and eventually remove it.

Step 10

Believe it or not, you really haven't even started chi kung practice yet. Everything so far has just been preparation! This is where it starts to get interesting. Chi kung exercise involves more than just standing. It involves engaging in a combination of physical relaxation and mental concentration that slowly begins to circulate the chi through your body.

This may be the point where your skepticism starts to kick in: "If I can't see chi, how do I know it really exists?" One way to begin to answer this is with a suggestion: Wiggle your left big toe. (I'll wait.)

OK, now. How did you do that? You didn't bend down and physically push and pull the toe with your fingers. And even if you did, how did you arrange to go through all of those complex motions? Scientists may be able to visually identify the combination of muscular contractions and even the nerve impulses that take place for you to wiggle your toe. They can even generate images of the impulses that occur in the brain that send these signals to the muscles and nerves. However, can anyone see, in any way, shape, or form, what triggered the brain to begin generating those signals? Absolutely not. Yet, we know that it happens. So it is with chi. You can't see it, but it happens.

In sum, just because you can't see all of the mechanisms that take place in your body to wiggle your left big toe doesn't mean that you aren't able to do so.

Here's how to get started moving your chi. As you stand in the proper position, focus on your abdomen. This is where chi is stored in the body (which is another reason a relaxed abdomen and abdominal breathing are so important to chi kung practice in specific and to life in general).

As you focus on your abdomen, it should gradually begin to get slightly warm. Once you begin to experience some of this warmth, gradually begin to "move" this warmth up the center of your body. Then, begin to move it down your arms to your hands, then back up.

The hands, in fact, tend to be among the most sensitive areas of the body in terms of the ability to feel chi. The reason is that the fingers are miniature bodies—complete with bones, muscle, fascia, and skin. As such, it is easy to move and feel chi in these areas. In fact, the fingers are usually the easiest places to feel chi. If you are practicing chi kung correctly, your fingers should become very warm.

Within a few minutes, your upper body as a whole should begin to feel warmer. You may begin to sweat. This is a sign that your chi is beginning to flow.

Work over the next several weeks at directing chi through your torso, arms, and hands. Why not the legs? For most people, the legs tend to be a difficult part of the body to direct chi. Eventually, though, you will be able to build up enough chi energy in the abdomen to gradually be able to direct it down and up the legs. You will know you have succeeded when you begin to feel warmth in your feet, and especially your toes. In fact, one of the early signs of overall bodily deterioration for people as they go through their lives is weakness and coldness in their lower legs, feet, and toes. This is a sign that their overall chi levels are weakening and that they are on a slow march toward death. Chi kung can help rebuild energy and vitality in the legs, feet, and toes.

Step 11

How long should you stay in the chi kung position? As long as you feel comfortable doing so. Most people, especially those who are out of shape, may only be able to stand for a couple of minutes. That's OK. Unlike the mentality of a lot of Western exercise promoters, which is, "No pain, no gain," and "Work it until it hurts," chi kung practice emphasizes slow and gentle energy building. As you practice each day, you will gradually be able to increase your time to fifteen minutes or more.

Before ending each session, cross the palms of your hands over your abdomen, and hold that position for a couple of minutes. Visualize the chi flowing from the torso downward to the abdomen, as well as directly from the arms and hands to the abdomen. This helps to store the chi back in the abdomen.

Experienced chi kung practitioners suggest that if you fail to engage in this storage phase, the chi will continue to circulate through the body and eventually diminish, defeating the purpose of chi kung practice, which is to build up your storehouse of chi.

Step 12

There are actually a dozen or more positions for "standing chi kung." The one described (hands relaxed at your sides) is the most common and the easiest to learn.

Another popular position is to hold both arms out straight in front of you, elbows slightly flexed, palms facing each other about one foot apart. If you eventually advance to this position, here is the sequence to follow:

1. Start with the "hands at the side" position for at least two minutes.

2. Move to the "hands out front" position and remain there as long as is comfortable.

3. Move back to the "hands at the side" position for at least two more minutes.

4. Move to the "palms over the abdomen" position for two minutes to end.

Chi Kung and Stress

So what does all of this have to do with stress? Chi kung practitioners over the last several thousand years have been using the practice to do a number of things. Among them are increase health, increase energy and endurance, maintain mental and emotional balance, and prevent stress.

In other words, by building up vitality and endurance in your body through chi kung practice, you can make it more and more immune to the emotional and physiological responses to stress.

I have been practicing chi kung on and off for almost ten years. I find that when I practice it on a regular basis (every night for a year or so), my life is virtually stress free, regardless of what circumstances occur around me. On the other hand, if I back-slide and practice sporadically or not at all for a couple of months, stress returns. It is at that time that I return to chi kung practice primarily as a way to reduce stress. Then, after practicing consistently for another month or two, its stress-prevention abilities kick back in.

Summary

In this chapter, you learned that chi kung is an exercise program designed to build and maintain healthy energy in your body. As you build energy through daily chi kung practice, your body, mind, and emotions begin to create more resilience to stress.

The basic practice of chi kung involves standing in a specific position for a period of time and allowing the energy in your body to move to all areas of your body. With practice, you will actually be able to direct the energy throughout your body. The final chi kung step involves collecting the energy again in your abdomen.

CHAPTER EIGHT

Meditation to Reduce Stress

As you will recall reading in Chapter 2,
at McGill University in Montreal in 1954, volunteers for an experiment were given twenty dollars a day (a decent sum back then) to lie in a bed with their basic needs being met.[1] However, the beds were in individual cubicles, and the volunteers' arms and hands were padded. In addition, they were required to wear goggles through which they could not see. Outside noise was masked by a speaker system. In sum, the volunteers were deprived of virtually all of their senses.

Most slept for the first few hours and enjoyed the relaxation. Soon, though, most began to experience boredom, restlessness, and anxiety. Some tried to stimulate themselves by singing, whistling, and talking to themselves, but nothing seemed to work. Gradually, more and more of the volunteers left their cubicles and resigned from the experiment. Most of them quit within twenty-four hours.

Eventually, those who did remain began to suffer from unsettling, and even terrifying, experiences and hallucinations. No one lasted beyond seventy-two hours.

To this day, this remains one of the most interesting studies on the subject of deprivational stress. It poses the question: Is physical, mental, and social isolation a source of stress for people, or a way to reduce stress? The answer is complex, and perspectives continue to be controversial, even fifty years after this landmark experiment.

In this chapter, we look at three individual, but related, topics: sensory deprivation, brain wave patterns, and meditation. The purpose is to show how, done properly, sensory deprivation combined with meditation can create a healthy combination of brain wave patterns that not only can reduce stress after the fact but, when practiced on a daily basis, can reprogram the brain to become resistant to the stress response.

Just as practicing chi kung (see Chapter 7) on a regular basis can make the body resistant to stress, practicing meditation on a regular basis can make the brain resistant to stress.

Sensory Deprivation

The book *Sensory Deprivation: Fifteen Years of Research* noted that long periods of isolation from other people have disturbing effects on people, as evidenced by the experiences of shipwrecked sailors, prisoners in solitary confinement, and individuals on long solo journeys.[2] Disturbances can include hallucinations and delusions. However, it requires a certain type of isolation to generate these experiences in people. The isolation being discussed is that in which there is no reduction in patterned stimulation, meaning that individuals still had the use of all five of their senses (sight, sound, touch, smell, and taste).

What effect does actual sensory deprivation have on people,

though? Sensory deprivation is isolation in which, as much as possible, access to sight, sound, touch, smell, and taste is denied. Another term for sensory deprivation is "deprivational stress." It is deemed to be the opposite of "overload stress." (Both concepts are discussed in detail in Chapter 2.)

Research into the effects of sensory deprivation on humans, while sporadically taking place as early as the 1930s, began in earnest in the early 1950s—the result of domestic fear over Communist methods that involved the brainwashing of American prisoners during the Korean War. The idea of the research was to study the effects of isolation and sensory deprivation on humans, then to find ways to help people overcome these negative experiences so they could be more resistant to brainwashing, were they ever to be subjected to it.

The experiments involved researchers attempting to remove as much sensory stimulation from human volunteers as possible and assessing the results in terms of emotional changes, intellectual changes, and physical changes. The two primary senses being controlled were vision (with volunteers being placed in total darkness) and hearing (with volunteers being prevented from hearing any sound). Less restricted was the sensation of touch, although volunteers often had their hands and feet placed in long arm and hand "cuffs" to limit tactile experiences. Some were even submerged in tanks filled with water. Food would be given on occasion, allowing for activation of the senses of taste and smell.

Several of the early experiments ended up having to be cut short because volunteers began experiencing frightening hallucinations, similar to what other people had reported about drug-induced hallucinations. Some volunteers began experiencing hallucinations within twenty minutes of being placed in isolation. Others survived for as long as seventy hours before experiencing them. Even most of those who did not report hallucinations experienced disorientation after being released (e.g., becoming lost on the way down the hallway to the washroom, something that had not been a problem prior to the experiment).

Others simply could not stand the solitude. One subject, who insisted on removing himself from the experiment early, reported leaving because "the quiet was so loud it was like a knife stabbing through my eardrums."[3]

The author of a 1956 experiment concluded:

> Isolation per se functions as a powerful stress on most people and often produces a variety of psychotic-like behaviors, including hallucinations, savior types of delusions, superstitiousness, intense love of any living things, conversations with inanimate objects, and a feeling that when one is once again among people he must be careful of what he says lest he be judged insane.[4]

Part of the reason for so many negative experiences during sensory deprivation experiments during the 1950s and 1960s was the fact that the general public knew well that the purpose of the experiments was to determine how well people could survive what was considered to be a negative experience (closely linked with Communist brainwashing).

As the Communist threat in general and the specific threat of brainwashing began to diminish in the 1960s, so did the intensely negative experiences of sensory deprivation. That is, during the 1950s, sensory deprivation tended to generate stress and disturbances. However, the reason was not the deprivation itself, but rather the attitude toward the deprivation, such as worrying about the loss of touch with reality.

This is evidenced by the fact that people didn't worry about loss of touch with reality when they slept every night at home, which was a form of sensory deprivation. People slept every night during the 1950s without anxiety related to the experience of sensory deprivation.

Subsequent studies on sensory deprivation seemed to shift from negative effects to neutral effects. Research became more detailed about why some people experienced negative effects and others did not. For example:

▶ Subjects exposed to sensory deprivation for the first time tended to have much more anxiety, stress, and negative experiences than did people who went through the experience a second time. One reason was that second-timers knew what to expect and realized that the experience in and of itself was not problematic. Attitude was the source of the anxiety and stress that led to the negative experiences.

▶ Those who were least willing to stay in sensory deprivation environments were those who required constant external stimuli—those who smoked and those who watched the most television. Those who stayed longest tended to be non-smokers and those who preferred reading books to watching television.

By the late 1970s, interest in sensory deprivation experiments had shifted from neutral to downright positive. There seem to be two reasons for this shift. First, by this time, funding for clinical experiments in sensory deprivation had all but dried up, because the government and public in general no longer feared "Communist brainwashing." Second, the pace of life was continuing to quicken, and people, rather than experiencing anxiety over sensory deprivation, were beginning to look for more and more ways to "get away from it all." In fact, around this time, flotation tanks became commercially available, allowing people to create their own sensory deprivation environments. These tanks allowed people to suspend themselves in completely enclosed tanks, where they could float in water for long periods of time. When people spent time in these immersion tanks, they often reported feelings of relaxation, restfulness, feelings of love, pleasant imagery, and even transcendental experiences (harmony with the universe, etc.).

One researcher, in fact, realizing that "dusk was falling" on sensory deprivation research, attempted to shift the focus from negative to positive by suggesting that a new term be used: *restricted environmental stimulation.*[5] In his book *Restricted Environmental Stimulation*, Peter Suedfeld pointed to the increased popularity of solitary activities such as cave exploring (spelunking), camping, hiking, and meditation.

In addition, prior to the "spiritual revolution," which began in the late 1970s, people equated conscious thinking and contact with the physical world as being the only reality, and the only way to maintain this contact was with the five senses. Being deprived of the opportunity to use the senses was seen as a frightening experience, because "reality" was being taken away, to be replaced by a frightening and unknown "nothingness." By the late 1970s, though, as people began to understand and identify more with the spiritual realm, new wisdom was suggesting that the physical world was an illusion, and that spiritual experiences constituted true reality. As such, sensory deprivation was an opportunity to leave the cacophony of the world and move toward genuine reality—the hallmark of which was genuine peace and enlightenment.

In other words, the idea of abandoning thought years ago was tantamount to losing touch with reality. Today, abandoning thought is viewed as the opportunity to move deeper into consciousness.

More and more people abandoned the belief that loss of senses and thought was a bad thing, a belief that was based on the idea that such surrender was taking one away from something safe, but toward nothing that was positive. As more people became interested in spiritual concepts, they realized that there was something beyond the real world—a spiritual world that had much to offer to them. As such, they saw things like sensory deprivation as ways to facilitate the transition from the real world to the spiritual world. Sensory deprivation was no longer a loss of control in the real world that led to a horrible, frightening, bottomless pit of darkness, but rather a portal to begin to experience the peace, joy, and fulfillment of the spiritual world.

In sum, sensory deprivation was seen not so much as an experience of losing reality but as a way to experience a new reality.

Suedfeld quoted from Thomas Merton, who said in 1957, "It is in silence, and not in commotion, in solitude and not in crowds, that God best likes to reveal himself most intimately to men."[6]

Brain Waves

The brain is constantly producing electrical impulses, which are measured in amplitude (power, measured in microvoltage) and frequency (speed, measured in cycles per second, or hertz). This is much the same way music is measured—amplitude is the volume or level of the sound (loudness), while frequency is the tone (deep bass through high-pitched sounds).

Of particular interest in understanding brain waves and their impact on the stress response is the frequency of the brain's electrical impulses, which determine the brain-wave pattern. There are four brain-wave patterns: beta (conscious), alpha (link between conscious and subconscious), theta (subconscious), and delta (unconscious). The combination of these waves in your brain at any one time determines your state of consciousness and your propensity for stress.

Beta. This is the highest-frequency series of brain waves, cycling at between thirteen and forty cycles per second. The brain produces beta waves in its normal waking state. When they are operating in an ideal environment, beta waves are capable of producing logical thinking, concrete problem solving, and active external attention. Excessive levels of beta, though, signal panic, anxiety, stress, and worry. This can also cause your heart and mind to race and your breathing to become short and shallow.

Alpha. This is the next highest frequency of brain waves, cycling at between eight and thirteen cycles per second. Alpha brain waves occur during daydreaming, fantasizing, and visualization. They are most frequently associated with relaxation, detached awareness, and a receptive mind.

For several years, people who studied brain waves falsely believed that the goal was to achieve a constant state of alpha, ignoring the important role of beta, theta, and delta and the important balance the four create together. For example, it has since been learned that excess-amplitude levels of alpha, at the expense of a combination of other brain waves, can lead to a life of chronic daydreaming and an unhealthy escape from reality. Today, experts understand that the most important role of alpha is to create a bridge between the conscious (beta) and the subconscious (theta).

Theta. This is the next highest frequency, cycling at between 4 and eight cycles per second. Theta brain waves are those that put you in touch with your intuition and with your subconscious. Theta brain waves, which can be activated during dream sleep and deep meditation, can lead to spiritual awakenings. These waves are also the primary source of creativity.

Delta. This is the lowest frequency, cycling at between 0.5 and 4 cycles per second. Delta waves are present during deep sleep, and it is these waves that provide the most restorative stages of sleep. Delta waves are also linked with intuition, the "sixth sense," and empathy for others (the ability to feel what others are feeling). In fact, people with excess levels of delta waves often feel themselves constantly barraged by emotional input from external sources.

The inability to easily access theta and delta waves often signals problems with insomnia.

Another problem occurs with people who have highly agitated minds. When they awake from the theta and delta waves associated with sleep, their minds, instead of transitioning slowly up to alpha waves, and then to beta, immediately shift into high-speed beta waves as they begin to think about and experience the stresses, worries, and anxieties of the coming day.

In her book *The High-Performance Mind*, Anna Wise uses the term *awakened mind* to refer to a balanced combination of the four brain waves, roughly characterized as moderate-amplitude levels of beta, theta, and delta, and a stronger-amplitude level of alpha.[7] It is important to note that any of the four brain waves can have low amplitudes, but for the awakened mind, all four brain waves must be activated to at least the moderate-amplitude level, with alpha even more active.

Alpha waves provide the bridge between the high-frequency beta and the extremely low-frequency delta. Without alpha, the conscious and unconscious are working but neither is aware of each other's activity. In addition, people sometimes utilize "alpha blocking" to prevent themselves from thinking about things they can't consciously handle (repressed memories, etc.).

What is important here to understand in terms of stress is that we can control brain-wave patterns much more easily, especially the middle waves (alpha and theta), when we are in a state of deep relaxation, which we can achieve through meditation.

Now that you have a background in the potential benefits of sensory deprivation and an understanding of brain waves, a discussion of meditation will make more sense.

Meditation

While meditation often has religious connotations for people, and while many religions, in both the East and West, have formal meditation practices, meditation, in its most simple and basic form, just means "getting quiet." It means trying to reduce the effects of the five senses on your brain, which then reduces the impact of the brain on the mind. With the mind less affected by directions from the brain, it is more free to relax and detach.

Meditation allows your mind to process stimuli from sources other than your five senses. It allows you to shut down the constant repetitive "clutter" and "chatter" that go through your mind all day, every day.

In one sense, meditation is a form of sensory deprivation. However, it is voluntary sensory deprivation, meaning that you can control how intensely you deprive your mind of your physical sensory experiences (i.e., how much you reduce sight, sound, smell, taste, and touch), as well as how long you deprive your mind of these experiences. That is, you can meditate for sixty seconds while sitting on a hard wooden bench in a park near a noisy playground on a bright, sunny day with a hot dog vendor five feet away. Or, you can meditate for thirty minutes while lying on a soft bed in a totally dark bedroom in a quiet neighborhood at midnight. (Experienced meditators can actually gain something from the former, although everyone will gain more from the latter.)

There are dozens of different ways to meditate, and each of these has numerous variations. In sum, it would take an encyclopedia to completely delineate all of the ways, steps, and substeps to meditate. The one I am outlining below is one that I have found particularly useful for keeping stress to a minimum in my life.

Step 1. While most books on meditation encourage you to sit in a chair with your back straight, it is possible to meditate just fine lying on a comfortable bed—or even on a carpeted floor. Find the position where you can get the most physically relaxed.

Step 2. As much as possible, block out surroundings that will affect your physical senses. That is, make the room as dark as possible. Find a place (and time) that will be as quiet as possible. Wear comfortable, nonbinding clothes.

Step 3. Close your eyes and begin to engage in abdominal breathing. Relax your body, letting go of as much muscle tension as you can.

Step 4. Become aware of the mental chatter that continues to take place in your mind. Don't attempt to forcefully suppress it. That would be an attempt to artificially try to dominate part of yourself, which would only build tension, pressure, and frustration. Instead, simply try to separate yourself from your thoughts. In other words, realize that you really do have two parts. If you don't believe me, consider these phrases that people use every day: "I told myself that . . ." "I was thinking to myself that . . ." When you use concepts like that, what you're really saying is that there are two parts to yourself—the "I" and the "myself." Another way to illustrate the concept is that you are able to have a conversation with yourself (talking to yourself). This is more than a monologue. It's a dialogue. There are two "you"s!

For the purposes of meditation, try to get in touch with the part of yourself that can simply observe and listen to the other part of yourself engage in its mental chatter. Lie back (or sit back) and become aware of that other entity—the Chatterbox. Don't try to control it. Just watch it and listen to it.

Step 5. Next, begin to get in touch with this new, separated entity—the quiet part of yourself—the observer. Stay with that experience for a couple of minutes. Continue to be aware that the other part of yourself—the Chatterbox—is still there, but it no longer dominates the scene. It has begun to fade into the background.

Step 6. Become the quiet entity, and begin to take a trip. Go somewhere that will be comfortable, relaxing, and peaceful for you. For some, this may be a sensation of floating up from Earth into outer space, where it is completely dark, quiet, and void. For others, it may mean lying on a beach. For others, it may mean being atop a mountain range overlooking acres of pine trees.

Beyond this point, there are a couple of options. Step 7A will delineate one of them. Step 7B will delineate the other.

Step 7A. One option is to simply stay with the quiet, relaxing experience, and allow your "quiet self" to go where it wants to go. Stay with the peaceful experience for as long as you wish, or until it ends on its own.

Step 7B. Another option is to begin to repeat what is called a "mantra"—or a sound that helps you continue to keep the chatter of your "first self" in the background. Some books on meditation suggest that you can select any sound or word that you wish, as long as it feels comfortable to you. In sum, you could repeat the word *chair* if it felt right. This, however, will get you nowhere. It is important to select a sound or word that contains the "ah" sound. The reason is that this sound resonates intensely in the body and creates the ideal vibrations for experiencing the

benefits of meditation. In fact, it's no coincidence that the majority of words for supreme beings and other spiritual leaders in
virtually every religion contains the "ah" sound: *God, Allah,
Buddha, Baal, Brahma,* and there are dozens more. Even thousands of years ago, people realized that the best way to get in
touch with their spiritual side was to repeat a word that con-
tained "ah" in it. If religions make you feel uncomfortable,
though, or you just find no use for them, you can repeat sounds
such as "hall" or even just "ah" itself.

There is no need to actually verbalize your phrase. Say it to
yourself quietly, or you can even just think it. Continue to do so
at a slow but steady pace until you reach a state of total relaxation. You may even get to bliss. This experience is difficult to
describe, but you'll know it once you experience it.

Step 8. Once you feel as though you have meditated long
enough (which may be as little as two minutes if you're just really
not able to get into it that day, or as long as thirty minutes),
allow yourself to come out of it slowly. Reconnect with the "real
world."

As you come out of meditation, your "other self" (the Chatterbox) will likely make its presence known again and take over
your mind. This is OK. By practicing meditation every day, or
especially twice a day, your "quiet self" will gradually begin to
gain more of a foothold, and your Chatterbox will gradually
begin to lose its grip and power. Eventually, your quiet self will
be the real you, and the Chatterbox will become nothing more
than a minor irritation or annoyance. If you eventually evolve to
a life of true peace, the Chatterbox will be nothing more than a
mild amusement to you.

In fact, this is where long-term meditation comes into play
as a stress-prevention strategy. Many people meditate occasion-

ally and sporadically as a way to reduce stress after the fact. If they have a stressful day, they will meditate to try to eliminate some of that stress. There's nothing wrong with this. It can work. If their day goes fine, they see no reason to meditate.

However, the real benefit of meditation is the long-term effect it has on the dominance of your Chatterbox self or your quiet self. When your Chatterbox rules your life, stress will continue to intrude into your life. The Chatterbox thrives on it. However, if you meditate each and every day, the quiet self will eventually become dominant, and the quiet self has no need for stress. Your perspective on life changes so much that stress becomes an alien presence that hovers on the periphery, rather than a natural part of your existence. It is an occasional intruder, not an integral part of your nature.

Summary

In this chapter, you learned that the concept of sensory deprivation, while once considered to be a frightening experience, can actually be a positive gateway to relaxation. You also learned that brain-wave patterns can determine your level of peace of mind. Finally, you learned that meditation is an effective way to help regulate these brain-wave patterns and ultimately help prevent the stress response from occurring as frequently in your life.

CHAPTER NINE

The Spiritual Road to Stress Prevention

If you have followed the suggestions in this book up through Chapter 6, you should be well on your way to reducing stress in your life. If you've also included the recommendations in Chapter 7 (chi kung exercises) and Chapter 8 (meditation), then stress will be an even more infrequent visitor.

If you find that what you have learned to this point has been sufficient to meet your needs, then you may feel like skipping Chapter 9. If so, that's fine, because this chapter is not for everyone.

For some people, Chapter 9 may be the single most important chapter for them in eliminating stress in their lives. For others, it may be additionally helpful. For still others, it may have no value at all. For some, it may have no value now, but, if you find yourself embarking on a spiritual journey in the years to come, you may want to revisit this chapter and find some value in it.

Spiritual Beliefs and Habits

The following recommendations are offered as additional ways to consider some important changes in your life. Feel free to select those that resonate with you. Ignore the others, but consider reassessing their possible value in the future.

Have Courage

In a medieval tale, a man feared taking the next step across a foggy chasm, because he could not see the step. He took the step anyway, with the faith that the step would be there. As he took the step, the fog parted, and there, indeed, was the next plank on the bridge for him to take. Invisible support always exists for you when you truly need it. You supply the courage to take the next step and move forward. The universe will provide the support you need.

Be Friends with Yourself

The ability to feel a sense of fulfillment and contentment while being alone is a sign of emotional maturity. In a culture in which social relationships are generally considered to provide the answer to every form of distress, it is sometimes difficult to persuade people that solitude can be as therapeutic, relaxing, and stress reducing as emotional support.

Give of Yourself

Research suggests that the most stress-resistant people also tend to be the most altruistic—those who engage in giving to others and caring for others. The theory is that when you take the focus off yourself and put it on others, there is less focus on your own stress.

Prioritize

Realize that nothing in this life matters. For example, Buckminster Fuller (1895–1983) was an inventor, architect, engineer, mathematician, and cosmologist who is best known as the inventor of the geodesic dome. At one time in his life, he contemplated suicide. Just as he was about to do so, he had an insight. He decided to live the rest of his life as if he were already dead. As such, everything he did and would do no longer had "weight" with it. He was free to do what he wanted. He realized that he was totally free, because nothing mattered. Some affirmations:

▶ *"In the long run, it doesn't really matter."*

▶ *"I don't sweat the small stuff. It's all small stuff."*

Focus on Spiritual Rewards

Engaging in worldly activities (shopping, watching TV, drinking, etc.) provides quick, easy, and tangible rewards, but these rewards are short term, artificial, and ultimately unsatisfactory.

Engaging in spiritual activities (meditation, walking, etc.) provides slow, challenging, and subtle rewards, but these rewards eventually become long term, genuine, and ultimately satisfactory.

It's similar to medicine. Many people prefer using pharmaceuticals, which provide immediate results, but have negative side effects and don't ever really address the source of the problem, which is some form of imbalance in the body. Other people prefer vitamins, minerals, and other natural supplements, which, *if taken properly,* rarely have negative side effects and eventually rebalance the body into health.

Indeed, you can spend a lot of time and energy focused on

worldly activities, where you can generate immediate gratification with little or no effort. However, the more time you spend nourishing your spirit, the less you will begin to crave worldly things and activities. The effects are similar to what happens when you make choices about food. If you live on junk food and don't exercise, you continue to crave junk food. However, if you make a conscious decision to begin to exercise and do what it takes to stay with the program, your body will gradually begin to crave healthy food to rebuild and nourish the muscles and other parts of the body that are becoming more healthy. After a while, you have no desire for junk food.

Eventually, you begin to realize that the real world is becoming less real and more of an illusion. The spiritual world becomes more real and less of an illusion.

From a personal perspective, I spent most of my life hooked on various things in the physical world. My primary addiction was collecting. I collected stamps and coins as a child. When I gave that up, I replaced it with collecting friends, then girlfriends. After I got married, I began collecting record albums and CDs. Each time I found something new to collect, I continued to hope that this would be "The Permanent Thing" that would ultimately make me happy. When it didn't, I would become disillusioned and then look for something else to collect.

Once I began to gain interest in spiritual experiences, though, I realized that external things are diversions from spirituality. Thus, any time I had a new compulsion to collect something or began to experience some other minor addiction, I stopped thinking of it as a potential salvation. Instead, I realized that it was a sign I was losing my grasp on spirituality. As such, I actually looked forward to my new desire ending so that I could begin to get back to my new spiritual reality. This, I realized, was the only thing that was permanent. In fact, it was not only permanent; it was permanently satisfying.

I also realized that each worldly addiction was a weak part of my personality that I needed to address. In other words, rather than looking toward it as a new salvation, I began to realize that my new temporary interest/addiction was giving me an opportunity to explore myself and address the personality weakness that it signified.

Find Peace—A Piece at a Time

Whether you realize it or not, you are two people. And until you do realize this, it will be difficult to find true peace and serenity in your life.

Imagine the following scenario: You're the parent of twin toddlers. One is loud, boisterous, frequently flustered, and always demanding. The other is quiet, reserved, relaxed, and not the least bit demanding. As a parent, how do you divide your time between the children? Many parents would devote the majority of their time to the first, with whatever time is left over for the second.

"This isn't fair to the second child," you are likely saying to yourself. "The second child deserves just as much attention."

There are two children in you. The worldly child is driven by your ego. This is the one who interacts with the world each day, encounters problems, and is constantly struggling for survival. Obviously, this is where you devote the majority of your attention—trying to keep this child afloat and sane.

However, hidden inside you is a second child—your "soul child" or "quiet child." This is the quiet part of you that can help you get in touch with your spiritual nature. Not only do few people spend time attending to this child; most people don't even realize it exists.

Find a way to spend some time with your quiet child each day. You may be able to do so by listening to relaxing music, taking a walk, meditating, or reading some inspirational passages from a book. Whatever it takes, get to know your quiet child.

Get Away from It All

Take a walk—in your own park. Can you hear the birds chirping in the trees? Can you hear the breeze blowing the tall grass in the field?

If you live in the country far from the noise and have managed to create a relaxing life for yourself, then you probably do hear the birds and breeze. However, if you live in an urban area, or even a suburban area, what you probably hear all day is traffic, industrial noise, jackhammers, people yelling, TVs, radios, and more.

So do you hear the birds and breeze? Probably not, but this doesn't mean the birds aren't chirping and the breeze isn't blowing. All it means is that you can't hear them.

If you were able to find a way to silence the traffic, the industrial noise, the jackhammers, the people yelling, the TVs, the radios, and everything else, you'd be surprised at the quiet beauty you would begin to hear. If you live in a city, there is probably a park somewhere nearby. Spend some time there.

You can also tune in the birds and breeze and visit the park metaphorically. Find time to just be quiet every day—to get within yourself. The more time you spend here, the more time you will want to spend here. Eventually, you may find more to value in your inner world than you will find in your outer world. If nothing else, the energy you gain from spending time in your inner world will serve you well when trying to cope with the outer world, and the "real problems" you face in your outer world won't seem so serious anymore.

Rely on the Spirit

Every problem, fear, and addiction has a solution in the spirit. Become peaceful and silent, and listen to God through meditation. You will be directed through the world of emotions to your inner divinity, where you can simply observe your emotions with detachment. Then, you will know what you truly need. The solution will come when you turn the problem over to the divine presence and then detach yourself from the problem and the solution. A problem cannot survive under these conditions. The universe will conspire to help you, since you are committed to wanting a solution, listening to the wisdom of God, and following His word. Two affirmations:

▶ *"I am never alone. God is always with me."*
▶ *"I cannot know fear once I know who walks beside me."*

Accept

Realize that things are as they should be. Adopt an attitude that "nothing goes wrong in my world." Do not identify with your problems. Do not "own" your problems. Problems are nothing more than natural comings and goings of the physical world. Watch problems around you, but do not become part of them, and do not allow them to become part of you.

Live in the Current Moment

You only need to do one thing at a time. Accept everything as it is. Every moment is as it should be. Two affirmations:

▶ *"Whatever happens is supposed to happen."*
▶ *"All is as it should be."*

Just "Be"

Some suggestions:

▶ Stop doing. Just be.

- Happiness and meaning are in being, not in doing.

- You can still do, and it can still be fun, but it does not bring happiness and peace of mind.

- Look for being, not doing, to bring you peace of mind.

- Don't look for meaning in doing. Look for meaning in being.

- Doing will always change. Being will be constant.

- Meaning is inside of you. It is who you are, not what you do.

Summary

In this chapter, you learned that looking at your world in a different way can totally change your perspective on stress. If you continue to view the physical world as reality, then there is a good chance stress will continue to be part of your life. On the other hand, if you can gradually shift your reality to that of the spiritual world, you will realize that experiences occurring in the physical world ultimately mean very little. As such, they are not important enough for you to bother experiencing stress.

PART IV

Your 100-Day Program

Although mastering stress management can be a lifelong endeavor, the following steps will get you started over the next 100 days. The real key, of course, is to integrate each activity or behavior into your life on a permanent basis. If you find that the rate of change suggested here is too rapid, slow it down to a pace that suits your abilities. Again, it is more important to adopt these recommendations as permanent habits than it is to rush through the program but fail to sustain the changes.

Part One—Sleep Strategies

Day 1. Make some specific changes in order to improve your ability to sleep better. Refer to Chapter 4 for specific tips.

Day 2. Reschedule your time in order to get enough sleep. This may mean putting off optional tasks until the weekend, delegating certain tasks to other family members (such as having the children do the dishes and cleaning up), and bypassing late-night television shows. (If there's one you just can't stand not to watch, tape it and watch it the following evening.)

Part Two—Improving Your Diet

Day 3. Begin to take a nationally recognized brand of multivitamin each morning. (Some of the vitamins and minerals generate energy, which could keep you awake if you take them in the evening.)

Days 4–5. Begin eating healthy food, especially increasing your servings of fruits, vegetables, whole grains, and cold-water fish (such as tuna, salmon, mackerel).

Day 6. Schedule a visit to your physician to discuss three topics:

1. Recommendations on how you can improve your diet

2. Whether he or she feels it is safe for you to take additional vitamins, minerals, and other supplements (refer to Chapter 4 for the list)

3. Clearance to begin an exercise program

Part Three—Reducing Bad Diet

Days 7–8. Cut back on salt. Check the salt content of the foods you normally eat, and cut back on extra salting of prepared meals.

Days 9–10. Cut back on refined sugars, such as donuts, candy, cakes, white bread, and soft drinks.

Days 11–12. Cut back on caffeine, especially coffee, but also soft drinks, chocolate, and tea.

Days 13–14. Cut back on alcohol, especially hard liquor and, to some extent, beer. If you still desire a drink, switch to red wine.

Day 15. Cut back on smoking, or give it up completely.

Part Four—Exercise and Relaxation

Days 16–18. If you receive the OK from your physician, begin a regular program of walking and/or using an exercise bike. One approach is to walk one day and bike the next. Increase to the point where you are walking one or two miles a day (twenty or thirty minutes) and biking for twenty to thirty minutes at a moderate pace the next day.

Days 19–21. Begin to breathe deeply at least four times per day (morning, afternoon, evening, before bed).

Days 22–24. Unplug the phone, lie on a bed or futon in the dark, close your eyes, relax your muscles, and engage in relaxed breathing for fifteen to twenty minutes.

Days 25–27. Begin a chi kung program.

Days 28–30. Begin a meditation program.

Part Five—Entertainment

Days 31–33. Cut way back on television. If your primary decision before was which channel button to press on the remote, replace that with a new decision of whether to press the on or off button. Only turn the television on if there is a specific program you really want to watch. Don't just lie there and "surf." For the programs that you do watch, focus on positive, life-affirming shows or comedies. Stay away from news, reality shows, "talking heads," dramas, cop shows, and all of the talk shows that parade a stream of fighting lowlifes across the stage.

Days 34–35. Become selective about the movies you go to or the videos you rent. Again, focus on comedies and/or those with positive, life-affirming messages.

Part Six—Communication

Days 36–37. Begin to journal. Write down the problems that you're experiencing, and allow the writing to take you where it wants. Don't force a specific direction. The results will be therapeutic.

Days 38–39. Arrange time to talk with a friend or family member on a regular basis to discuss concerns, problems, stresses, worries, etc. Don't force someone into the position of being your "human dumping ground" or bore them with the same problems over and over. If this is what you feel you need to do, though, hire a counselor.

Part Seven—Changing Your Assessment of the Situation

Activities in this part are intentionally scheduled to take longer, since changing attitudes is nothing you can easily do overnight.

Days 40–43. Focus on knowledge. Make an effort to spend less time with negative people who are always telling you how terrible life and the world are, and why you should be as miserable as they are.

Days 44–47. Focus on responsibility. If you find yourself getting stressed out frequently because you take on responsibility for issues that are not your responsibility, let go and allow those who are responsible for them to handle them. Make yourself available to these people if they need assistance, but insist that they take primary responsibility.

Days 48–51. Focus on conscientiousness. Although you don't want to give up being conscientious (it is a good quality!), consider each task you are facing and ask just how conscientious you need to be. Allow your rational self to triumph over your emotional self.

Days 52–55. Focus on what you care about and value. Assess each situation and determine whether it is appropriate to care. Then, stop caring about situations where there is no need to do so.

Days 56–59. Focus on enjoyment. Begin a habit of being more open to experiences. By taking the time to explore a subject or experience with an open mind, you may be able to shift from a "don't like" to a "neutral" attitude, or a "neutral" attitude to a "like" attitude.

Days 60–63. Focus on control. Begin with small steps. If you're in a situation where you feel you have no control, pretend that you do. Try something that you have never tried before. See what happens.

Days 64–67. Focus on situational competence. Remember that competence is a function of actual competence and perceived competence. When you challenge yourself in a situation where you feel incompetent, you may find that you are at least a bit more competent than you thought.

Part Eight—Changing Your Assessment of Yourself

Days 68–71. Focus on general life competence. Refer to recommendations in Chapter 5 and implement those that make sense. Then, begin using one or more of these affirmations:

▶ *"I am competent. I make good decisions."*

▶ *"Security is handling things, not having things."*

▶ *"Whatever happens, I can handle it."*

Days 72–75. Focus on active courage. Again, refer to recommendations in Chapter 5 and implement those that make sense. Then, begin using one or more of these affirmations:

▶ *"I enjoy expanding my comfort zone."*

▶ *"I enjoy challenging situations."*

Days 76–79. Focus on passive courage. Again, refer to recommendations in Chapter 5 and implement those that make sense. Then, begin using one or more of these affirmations:

▶ *"Safety is the presence of courage, not the absence of danger. I trust in my ability to survive."*

▶ *"I only need enough courage to face the current moment."*

▶ *"I will, after all, survive every moment but my last."*

Days 80–83. Focus on flexibility. Again, refer to recommendations in Chapter 5 and implement those that make sense. Then, begin using one or more of these affirmations:

▶ *"I enjoy new situations."*

▶ *"I behave as appropriate for the situation."*

Days 84–87. Focus on humor. Again, refer to recommendations in Chapter 5 and implement those that make sense. Then, begin using one or more of these affirmations:

▶ *"I enjoy life."*

▶ *"Life is fun."*

▶ *"I enjoy laughing."*

Days 88–91. Focus on optimism. Again, refer to recommendations in Chapter 5 and implement those that make sense. Then, begin using one or more of these affirmations:

▶ *"I keep problems in perspective. I compartmentalize."*

▶ *"Everything that enters my life helps me in some way."*

▶ *"Every adversity has the seed of an equal or greater benefit."*

▶ *"What's good about this?"*

Days 92–95. Focus on hardiness. Again, refer to recommendations in Chapter 5 and implement those that make sense. Then, begin using the following affirmation:

▶ *"That which does not kill me makes me stronger."*

Part Nine—Embracing Spirituality

Days 96–100. Reread Chapter 9 and select an activity to implement that is relevant and meaningful to you.

And finally, remember: That which does not kill you does make you stronger. Stress can kill you, or you can use stress to make you stronger. I hope this book helps you achieve success, happiness, fulfillment, and peace of mind with the latter.

Notes

Introduction

1. AdvancePCS, "AdvancePCS Study Shows Decline in Productivity Following Terrorist Attacks: Scope of Impact Is Nationwide," Press release, 30 October 2001.

2. Lori Joseph and Keith Simmons, "Many Often Feel Stress," *USA Today*, 24 January 2002, sec. A, p. 1.

Chapter One

1. Donald DeCarlo, "More on Workplace Stress," *Risk & Insurance*, 1 October 2001, p. 10.

2. Steven Sauter et al., "Stress at Work," National Institute for Occupational Safety and Health (NIOSH), NIOSH publication 99-101, 1999.

3. Ibid.

4. The American Institute of Stress, "Job Stress," The American Institute of Stress. http://www.stress.org/job.htm.

5. Ibid.

6. Ibid.

7. Joanne Wojcik, "Stress: A Major Risk," *Business Insurance*, 19 April 1999, p. 18.

8. Ibid.

9. The American Institute of Stress, "Job Stress," The American Institute of Stress. http://www.stress.org/job.htm.

10. Elizabeth L. Bland, et al., "19 Years Ago in *TIME*," *TIME*, 11 March 2002.

11. Joanne Wojcik, "Stress: A Major Risk," *Business Insurance*, 19 April 1999, p. 18.

12. Thomas T. Perls, Margery Hutter Silver, and John F. Lauerman, *Living to 100: Lessons in Living to Your Maximum Potential at Any Age* (New York: Basic Books, 1999), pp. 65–68.

13. Deepak Chopra, M.D., *Ageless Body, Timeless Mind: The Quantum Alternative to Growing Old* (New York: Harmony Books, 1993), p. 153.

14. Time-Life Books, *Managing Stress: From Morning to Night* (Alexandria, Virginia: Time-Life Books, 1987), p. 16.

15. Catherine M. Stoney et al., "Acute Psychological Stress Reduces Plasma Triglyceride Clearance," *Psychophysiology* 39 (January 2002): pp. 80–85.

16. Jean Carper, *Your Miracle Brain* (New York: HarperCollins, 2000), pp. 28–29.

17. Elissa Epel et al., "Stress and Body Shape: Stress-Induced Cortisol Secretion Is Consistently Greater Among Women with Central Fat," *Psychosomatic Medicine* 62 (September/October 2000): pp. 623–632.

18. Deepak Chopra, M.D., *Ageless Body, Timeless Mind: The Quantum Alternative to Growing Old* (New York: Harmony Books, 1993), pp. 166–167.

19. Robert M. Sapolsky, *Why Zebras Don't Get Ulcers: An Updated Guide to Stress, Stress-Related Diseases, and Coping* (New York: W.H. Freeman & Co., 1998), pp. 195–209.

20. Time-Life Books, *Managing Stress: From Morning to Night* (Alexandria, Virginia: Time-Life Books, 1987), p. 15.

21. Timothy McCall, M.D., "Get a Healthier, Frazzle-Free, Life," *Redbook*, September 2001, p. 28.

22. Robert S. Eliot and Dennis L. Breo, *Is It Worth Dying For?: A Self-Assessment Program to Make Stress Work for You, Not Against You* (New York: Bantam Books, 1984), pp. 15–16.

23. G. L. Engel, "Emotional Stress and Sudden Death," *Psychology Today* 11 (1977): pp. 115–121.

Chapter Two

1. Thomas Holmes and Richard Rahe, "Social Readjustment Rating Scale," *Journal of Psychosomatic Research* 11 (1967): pp. 213–218.

2. Phillip Rice, *Stress and Health* (Pacific Grove, California: Brooks/Cole Publishing, 1992), p. 68.

3. Al Siebert, telephone interview, 4 August 2000.

Chapter Three

1. William Atkinson, "Supply Chain Stress," *Purchasing Magazine*, 18 October 2001, pp. 20–21.

2. Daniel Girdano, George Everly, Jr., and Dorothy Dusek, *Controlling Stress and Tension: A Holistic Approach* (Boston: Allyn & Bacon, 1997), p. 139.

3. Steven Sauter et al., "Stress at Work," National Institute for Occupational Safety and Health (NIOSH), NIOSH publication 99-101, 1999.

4. Joel Goodman, telephone interview, 16 August 2000.

5. Martin Seligman, Ph.D., *Learned Optimism* (New York: Knopf, 1991).

6. Walt Schafer, Ph.D., *Stress Management for Wellness* (Fort Worth: Harcourt Brace Jovanovich, 1996), p. 160.

7. Thomas T. Perls, Margery Hutter Silver, John F. Lauerman, *Living to 100: Lessons in Living to Your Maximum Potential at Any Age* (New York: Basic Books, 1999), pp. 65–68.

Chapter Four

1. National Sleep Foundation, "Less Fun, Less Sleep, More Work: An American Portrait," Press release, 27 March 2001.

2. D. E. Kripke et al., "Short and Long Sleep and Sleeping Pills: Is Increased Mortality Associated?" *Archives of General Psychiatry* (1999): pp. 103–116.

3. Michael T. Murray, *Stress, Anxiety, and Insomnia: How You Can Benefit from Diet, Vitamins, Minerals, Herbs, Exercise, and Other Natural Methods* (Rocklin, California: Prima Publishing, 1995), pp. 66–67.

4. Time-Life Books, *Managing Stress: From Morning to Night* (Alexandria, Virginia: Time-Life Books, 1987), p. 21.

5. Ibid., pp. 23–24.

6. Deepak Chopra, M.D., *Ageless Body, Timeless Mind: The Quantum Alternative to Growing Old* (New York: Harmony Books, 1993), pp. 166–167.

7. Time-Life Books, *Managing Stress: From Morning to Night* (Alexandria, Virginia: Time-Life Books, 1987), p. 22.

8. Timothy McCall, M.D., "Get a Healthier, Frazzle-Free, Life," *Redbook*, September 2001, p. 34.

Chapter Five

1. Al Siebert, Ph.D., *The Survivor Personality: Why Some People Are Stronger, Smarter, and More Skillful at Handling Life's Difficulties . . . And How You Can Be, Too* (New York: Perigee Publishing, 1996), pp. 27–30.

2. Martin Seligman, Ph.D., *Learned Optimism* (New York: Knopf, 1991).

Chapter Six

1. Carl G. Jung, *Psychological Types* (1921; reprint, Princeton, New Jersey: Princeton University Press, 1976).

Chapter Eight

1. Phillip Rice, *Stress and Health* (Pacific Grove, California: Brooks/Cole Publishing, 1992), p. 68.

2. John Zubek, ed., *Sensory Deprivation: Fifteen Years of Research* (New York: Appleton-Century-Crofts, 1969), p. 7.

3. Philip Solomon et al., eds., *Sensory Deprivation: A Symposium Held at Harvard Medical School* (Cambridge, Massachusetts: Harvard University Press, 1961), p. 85.

4. Duane Schultz, *Sensory Restriction: Effects on Behavior* (New York: Academic, 1965), p. 148.

5. Peter Suedfeld et al., *Restricted Environmental Stimulation: Research and Clinical Applications* (New York: Wiley, 1980), pp. 3–4.

6. Ibid., p. 202.

7. Anna Wise, *The High-Performance Mind: Mastering Brainwaves for Insight, Healing, and Creativity* (New York: Putnam, 1995), p. 10.

Index

About the Author

William Atkinson has been a full-time freelance writer since 1976. His specialty areas are writing about workplace safety and health, human resources, and employee relations issues. He holds a bachelor's degree in social studies from Southern Illinois University (1973) and a master's degree in business communication, also from SIU (1982). This is his seventh book.

He began researching stress in 1979. Since that time, he has interviewed numerous national experts on stress and related topics such as human resilience, optimism and pessimism, learned helplessness, risk-taking behaviors, alternative medicine, meditation, chi kung, and diet and exercise. He has written over three dozen magazine articles on stress from a number of different perspectives.

Atkinson lives in Carterville, Illinois, with his wife Johna, daughter Krista, and son John. His hobbies include exercising, reading, listening to progressive electronic music, watching spiritually uplifting movies, and investing in high-risk international equities.